How to Become a Nonprofit Rockstar:

50 Ways to Accelerate Your Career

How to Become a Nonprofit Rockstar

50 Ways to Accelerate Your Career

Rosetta Thurman

&

Trista Harris

Acknowledgements

From Rosetta

For my mother (Kimberly Linton) and grandmother (Tennie Mae Thurman), who made it possible for me to grow into the kind of woman who could choose a life of passion and purpose. And my grandfather (Clarence Noble), who constantly reminded me of his unwavering love. May he rest in endless peace.

Thank you to all the amazing nonprofit bosses and mentors I've had over the years like Chuck Bean, Amanda Marshall, and Robert Egger. I continue to draw from your wisdom in my life and work.

Thank you to all my blog readers who have supported me over the four years. You inspire me daily with your stories and thoughtful insight.

And thank you, a million times over, to the beautiful ones who get up every day and choose love over fear, to do the incredible and important work that everyone else has deemed impossible. You all are my heroes and sheroes in this difficult but rewarding journey to make a positive impact on the world.

From Trista

Special thanks to my husband Mark, who always encourages me to dream the impossible dream. I have endless gratitude for my children, Nia and Marcus, who have planted the seed of determination in me to make the world a better place for them and their children's children. I'd also like to thank my dad (Don Carter), my mom (Constance White), and my stepdad (Jerry White) for supporting my decision to go into a career in nonprofits, even though they were sure from the title of the sector that I would never make a profit.

Thank you to all of my mentors. Just a few are listed here but there are hundreds more that have helped me along the journey: Wiley Scott, Merline Ballard, Dr. Horace Dawson, Claire Chang, Rusty Stahl, Dr. Sam Myers, Gary Cunningham, Sherece West, The ABFE Fellows, Athena Adkins, Vickie Williams, Sara Lueben, Ben Jealous, EPIP-MN, and The Fab 5. A special thank you to the board and staff of the Headwaters Foundation, you have showed me the power of being a catalyst for social change.

Last but not least, I would like to thank the readers of my blog, New Voices of Philanthropy. I thought blogging would be a solitary activity, where I could get some of my thoughts about the generational transfer of leadership recorded. What I didn't realize is that my blog would give me a fabulous, international network of support and encouragement. You are some of the smartest, most idealistic people that I have ever met, in-person and virtually. You make me confident that the work of the social sector will only get better and better.

Rosetta and Trista would also like to acknowledge the great work of YNPN and EPIP. YNPN and EPIP are two fabulous organizations that you need to know about and that need to know about you. We highlight their work because they share our passion for supporting and nurturing young nonprofit and philanthropic professionals.

YNPN

YNPN is a national 501(c)3 grassroots nonprofit organization that engages and supports current and future nonprofit leaders through professional development, networking, and social opportunities.

Founded in 1997 as a small gathering of peers in San Francisco, the Young Nonprofit Professionals Network (YNPN) has become the largest grassroots network of young professionals in the sector. The network currently serves 20,000 members via over 30 local chapters across the U.S., including our charter chapters in the San Francisco Bay area, Denver, Chicago, New York City, and Washington, DC.

The mission of YNPN is to promote an efficient, viable, and inclusive nonprofit sector that supports the growth, learning, and development of young professionals. We accomplish this by providing members with local professional development opportunities, networking, educational workshops, and social programming as well as advocacy and partnerships on a national level. In 2009 alone, YNPN chapters provided over 300 high impact professional development events in over 15 states to an estimated 6,000 members.

YNPN chapters offer plentiful opportunities to learn about the nonprofit sector in your community, build your network, connect to local resources, and take on leadership roles and projects as a volunteer. To get involved in a YNPN chapter in your community or to learn more about their work, check out www.ynpn.org.

EPIP

The mission of Emerging Practitioners in Philanthropy (EPIP) is to strengthen the next generation of grantmakers in order to advance effective social justice philanthropy.

In 2001, EPIP was founded by a small group of young foundation professionals and individual donors who sought to work and learn with peers in order to transform philanthropy and confront generational issues in the social change community.

EPIP members are professionals at foundations, government and corporate grant-making entities, and philanthropy support organizations (such as regional associations of grantmakers, affinity groups, and financial advisory firms). Some members are foundation trustees, or donors involved in giving circles and other forms of organized giving. Graduate students studying philanthropy are also welcome. EPIP does not discriminate by age, but because we were started by and for young professionals, our constituents are generally under forty years of age. Members range from weeks to years of work in this field, and from program associates to presidents in terms of responsibility.

EPIP offers networking opportunities through local chapters and national convenings, as well as programming to strengthen the leadership and advocacy skills of its membership. To get involved with an EPIP chapter in your community or to learn more, visit www.epip.org.

Table of Contents

Chapter 1: What a Nonprofit Career Path Looks Like 1

There is No Linear Career Path 1
Rosetta's Journey 2
Trista's Journey 4
How Do You Get from Here to There? 6

Chapter 2: Develop Expertise 9

Tip 1: Find a Great Nonprofit Job 9
Tip 2: Size Matters 14
Tip 3: Make the Most of Your Volunteer Experience 19
Tip 4: Learn How to Raise Money 21
Tip 5: Always Learn, Always Teach 24
Tip 6: Work Abroad 27

Chapter 3: Build a Strong Network 29

Tip 7: Prioritize Networking 29
Tip 8: Attend Nonprofit Conferences 30
Tip 9: Get Your Own Business Cards 31
Tip 10: Join Professional Associations 32
Tip 11: Go Talk to People 34
Tip 12: Build Your Own Frankenmentor 39
Tip 13: Start Your Own Network 43

Chapter 4: Establish a Great Personal Brand 45

Tip 14: Google Yourself 46
Tip 15: Stop Trying to be Two Different People 48
Tip 16: Write a Kick-butt Bio 51
Tip 17: Professionalize Your Online Presence 53
Tip 18: Start a Blog 54
Tip 19: Look Like a Leader 59

Chapter 5: Practice Authentic Leadership 63

Tip 20: Do Your Job and Do it Well 63
Tip 21: Join a Nonprofit Board of Directors 66

Tip 22: Lead a Committee 69
Tip 23: Cultivate a Slash Career 73
Tip 24: Polish Your Public Speaking Skills 75
Tip 25: Ask for Feedback.......................................81
Tip 26: Do a Stretch Assignment 81
Tip 27: Speak Up! 84
Tip 28: Mentor Someone Else...................................86

Chapter 6: Plan for Balance.. 89

Tip 29: Develop a Personal Mission Statement................89
Tip 30: Schedule Time to Reflect..............................91
Tip 31: Don't Skip Lunch 93
Tip 32: Fall Back in Love With Your Job 94
Tip 33: Ditch the Martyr Lifestyle 96
Tip 34: Clear Off Your Plate 98
Tip 35: Mind Your Money 101
Tip 36: When Work and Home Collide 104

Chapter 7: Move On Up 109

Tip 37: Create Your Own Professional Development Plan. 109
Tip 38: Set Big Goals... 110
Tip 39: Get a Master's Degree................................ 113
Tip 40: Manage Up 117
Tip 41: Get Paid What You are Worth........................ 120
Tip 42: Consider the Benefits 123
Tip 43: Get Promoted 125
Tip 44: Introduce Yourself to a Search Firm 127
Tip 45: Use Your Network to Find a New Job 135
Tip 46: Get an Executive Coach.............................. 136
Tip 47: Know When to Take the Leap 140
Tip 48: Resign Gracefully 143
Tip 49: Be a Good Manager 144
Tip 50: Run with the Big Dogs 148

Resources...154

Books You Should Totally Read............................... 154
Professional Associations Worth Joining 155
Foundation and Nonprofit Fellowships We Love 159

Introduction

There is no lonelier place then the back corner of a ballroom during a nonprofit conference. There are tables of people chatting with each other, exchanging business cards, and sharing the latest nonprofit gossip. All of this is happening while you sulk at the table in the very back of the ballroom alone. You think, "I hate these things. I could be at the office working on my mountain of paperwork." You start playing with the hole in your nylons and use your conference issued pen as a pin for your bun. You see your idiot boss a few tables up, yucking it up with one of your organization's board members. Your fists ball up as you remember your performance review from last week. You had expected a decent raise and a promotion because you've been working 60-hour weeks for the last two years. It didn't happen and now you feel more stuck than ever. This is not what you expected when you signed up for your first nonprofit job. Your college career counselor had said that with your brains and passion for making the world a better place, you would do well in the nonprofit sector. "Yeah, if anyone noticed either of those things about me," you think.

Then you see her walk in. You see her at all of these things and every time it makes your stomach drop in envy. She's always so fabulous. Her hair looks like it should be on the head of someone in a shampoo commercial. She's wearing a gorgeous suit that is professional but doesn't feel like you would see a rack of them at the mall, and she is smiling and waving at various colleagues as she goes to her seat at the front of the room. You think, "What is she? Three minutes older than me? Yet she is a VP for that super innovative tutoring program that nobody can stop talking about and wherever she goes people treat her like some sort of nonprofit rockstar." Just then, she gets up from her seat and approaches the podium. She gives a stirring introduction for the lunch's keynote speaker and the people at the tables around you can't stop taking about how wonderful she is. You sink down in your chair and wish that your career was going just one-tenth as well as hers is.

If you have ever been that person in the back corner of a ballroom, we feel your pain. We've both spent too long being frustrated about the pace of our careers and jealous of others' success. We wrote this book because we were able to figure out how to make our own careers soar, and we want the same for you in your nonprofit career.

Just to give you an idea of why this is so important, let's take a look at the stats.

In 2008, a Meyer Foundation report found that one in three emerging nonprofit leaders aspires to be an executive director someday, yet only 4 percent of them are explicitly being developed to become their organization's executive director. And of that 4 percent, women are being developed at a lower rate than men.

Our solution? Give nonprofit professionals an accessible, do-it-yourself map of how to navigate the sector and the tools they need to move from entry-level positions to leadership roles. There are a number of books out there about how to get a nonprofit job, but very few on how to advance once you get there. The current nonprofit career advice books on the market are either geared toward first-time job-seekers or sector-switchers. In contrast, *How to Become a Nonprofit Rockstar* is a guide for current nonprofit employees who have already been in the sector for a few years and are looking for ways to get ahead in their careers.

This book is designed to give you 50 different tips that you can use to start changing the trajectory of your nonprofit career. You'll learn tangible lessons and hear from some of the nonprofit rockstars you've been envying from the back of the ballroom. You're just as smart as they are, just as ambitious as they are, and have a similar education background. The difference is that they have taken the additional step of branding themselves and proactively managing their careers. It's an important step that you can take too. We're looking forward to helping you start this journey and can't wait to see how it changes your career for the better!

Chapter 1: What a Nonprofit Career Path Looks Like

There is No Linear Career Path

One of the biggest frustrations that nonprofit professionals have is that there is no linear career path in the nonprofit sector. In most industries, there's a clear path to leadership positions in your organization. In many companies, you might start out as an assistant, and then get promoted to manager, then director, then VP, then senior VP, then hopefully one day the President if you have the ambition to be so. But in nonprofits, there is no clear journey to a promotion.

We love to read stories like that of Ursula Burns, the new CEO of Xerox who first came to the company as a summer intern in 1980. It wasn't until 30 years later that she came to hold the incredible title of being the first African-American woman to lead a major U.S. corporation.

Thirty years is a long time. Too long, if you ask us. In the nonprofit world, you could stay at a job for five years and never move up from your program associate position. Most of the time, though, it's not because you're not a rockstar program associate, but because you work for a small nonprofit and there's just no other position in the organization to which you can be promoted. It's times like these that young workers either get discouraged or get creative. If you really want to be happy in your nonprofit job, we suggest the latter. The great thing about working in the nonprofit sector is that you don't have to wait that long to become the head of an organization, if that's what you want to do. In nonprofits, there *is* no linear career path, which means that if you innovate your nonprofit career, you can lead whenever you're ready to. The slate is blank for you to get in where you fit in, wherever you think you can do some good. So without further ado, allow us to introduce ourselves.

Rosetta's Journey

In order for you to understand why I'm so passionate about social change and the nonprofit sector, you have to know a little bit more about my background. Sure, my requisite bio will tell you that I have had quite a bit of higher education and nonprofit work experience. What I also mention is that I grew up in the public housing projects near Cleveland, Ohio. My mother was a single teenage parent and my father was a drug dealer. He died when I was six and sure didn't leave an inheritance. My family didn't just "not have a lot of resources"; we were poor. We were so poor that every year, a woman from a local nonprofit would come and take me shopping for school clothes because my mother could not afford to.

Fast-forward through grade school and many kind teachers, afterschool programs, and special enrichment classes, and I became the first person in my family to graduate from college. But there was always this tug that kept getting stronger and stronger that I had to do something to help other people succeed in life. Otherwise, what was I here for? That feeling is what led me to volunteer at local afterschool programs as a reading tutor when I was in college. It was philanthropy that had provided an enhanced education for me as a child. It was nonprofits that had come to our aid when we couldn't make ends meet. It was philanthropy that had helped me to pay for college. Somebody did it for me, and I wanted to help someone else. That's how I got introduced to the nonprofit world and have known that's where I am called to do my life's work ever since.

After I graduated from college with a bachelor's degree in English, I found my first full-time nonprofit job on the Idealist.org website. It was the perfect job for me in the beginning of my nonprofit career. Luckily, I had already been working in the nonprofit field for almost three years on a part-time basis doing grantwriting and communications work for a few small community development agencies. I had no idea, however, whether I could even find a full-time job that wouldn't leave me homeless since the luxury of financial aid was long gone. My apprehension was heightened because I had also chosen to relocate from Richmond, Virginia, where I went to college, to Washington, DC, where all the nonprofits were, according to my professors. I had no friends in DC and no money. All I knew was that I wanted a nonprofit job.

My first attempt was to go through a temp agency where I landed a great administrative position at United Way. But it just wasn't the right fit for me and I left after just a few months to continue my search for the perfect nonprofit position.

What happened next is that I found an open position with an organization in DC that worked with youth-serving organizations in communities of color. I had volunteered with African-American youth in college. I cared deeply about people of color and how nonprofits could serve us. This was perfect for me; I can't tell you how badly I wanted this job. Yet they didn't even call me until a month after I had applied!

Then, all of a sudden, I had an interview with them at 2:00 p.m. I got lost on the way there because I still hadn't figured out the DC subway system. I was late. I thought I'd blown it. But they called to offer me the job at 5:00 p.m. that same day. And the rest, as they say, is history.

Since then, I've been working in the nonprofit community for the past eight years within the fields of youth development, historic preservation, capacity building, and membership associations. I hold a master's degree in Organizational Management with a concentration in Nonprofit Management from Trinity Washington University and a bachelor's degree in English from Virginia Commonwealth University. I've also completed advanced training programs at The Fund Raising School at the Center on Philanthropy at Indiana University and the Institute for Nonprofit Management at Columbia Business School. Given my English major background, my nonprofit roles have mostly focused on grantwriting and fundraising. My last position was Director of Development and Special Programs at the Nonprofit Roundtable of Greater Washington.

But this is how my career *really* took off. In 2007, I started a blog (Perspectives from the Pipeline, as it was called then) and quickly gained an audience for my ideas about nonprofit leadership from the perspective of a young person of color in the sector. Building my personal brand through blogging quickly afforded me some amazing leadership opportunities such as speaking engagements, an adjunct position at a local university, nonprofit board membership, and being named a "New Leader in Philanthropy" by Greater DC Cares. I was also invited to travel around the country and consult with nonprofits around how to approach intergenerational leadership issues, promote racial diversity, and tell their stories using social media.

Ultimately, my success in using social media to build my personal brand is what allowed me to make the decision to leave my job and branch out into full-time nonprofit consulting in January 2010. I am now the president of my own firm, Thurman Consulting, which provides speaking, training, coaching and consulting services for nonprofits, foundations, and socially responsible companies.

I wrote this book with Trista because over the years, I've heard from hundreds of young nonprofit professionals who struggle to make themselves visible in a sector that doesn't always grant them the respect they deserve. The good news? By using even just a few of the strategies we suggest, your career can go from 0 to 60 in a very short amount of time. I promise.

Trista's Journey

My stomach was doing flip flops. I was standing on a stage under blinding lights. I could make out just a small part of the crowd but knew that there were more than 300 nonprofit executives staring at me. I could hear the MC making jokes with the Governor's candidate-turned-private foundation President (responsible for $600 million in assets) and knew that I was next. More butterflies. "Next we have Trista Harris, Executive Director of the Headwaters Foundation for Justice." I reminded myself that this was the moment I had been preparing for as long as I could remember. It was time to get over myself and enjoy the moment. I stepped forward and tried to remember that the "meet the new foundation CEOs" event was supposed to be fun.

I'm always surprised when people say I am so young to be the executive director of a foundation. I've been preparing for this position for the last 25 years. Most kids in second grade draw pictures of ponies or their dream house. I used to draw floor plans of community centers. When I was about eight years old my mom started volunteering as a costume designer for a local theater. She brought me with her to the practices that took place at a local community center. I had lots of time to explore all the nooks and crannies there, and I remember being so impressed with all the services offered there. From then on, I was positive that I wanted to work for a nonprofit organization.

In high school, I worked as a coach at a neighborhood park, fundraised for youth groups, became a Big Sister as soon as I could, and pushed all of my friends to volunteer at the local Boys and Girls Club. I went to college at Howard University in Washington, DC, and loved the national think tanks and large-scale nonprofits. A career in nonprofits didn't feel like an option, it felt like a calling. A master's degree in Public Policy with a focus on Nonprofit Management sealed the deal.

Even with all that preparation, after a year into my first real job as a grantwriter, I felt stuck. There wasn't a clear career path and I could see how easy it would be to do this job for 15 years and never grow. I was too shy to network and I felt like there were secret rules to how my organization operated that I just didn't understand. I had all these ideas about how to improve our processes and how to make a bigger impact in communities of color, but I felt like no one would listen to me because of my title. I also felt frustrated because I thought my salary was too low for the work that I was doing.

Luckily, I was introduced to a fundraising consultant and he offered me some contract grantwriting work. With him, I learned that the skills that I had were valuable and that I could make money outside of a 9-to-5 job. Eventually, one of the organizations that I was writing grants for hired me as their Director of Advancement. I suddenly had a seat at the table and my voice was heard. I felt like I was making a real impact at the organization and my confidence in my own abilities grew. A position as a program officer at a wonderful community foundation soon followed. Because foundation positions are often seen as the last stop before retirement, I was 10 to 30 years younger than my peers and realized that generational challenges would be the next mountain to climb. I co-founded Minnesota's Emerging Practitioners in Philanthropy (EPIP) Chapter and developed an amazing network of peers that encouraged my professional development, helped me stretch my leadership skills, and increased my visibility exponentially. My blog New Voices of Philanthropy was a natural outgrowth of my work with EPIP and has been so important in helping me develop a network of colleagues across the country.

When the Executive Director position came open at the Headwaters Foundation for Justice, I refused to get my hopes up. The position was just too perfect and too aligned with my skills and passion. I knew that I couldn't expect to get a job that wonderful for another 10 years and was hesitant to even apply. I greatly credit my network for encouraging me to apply for the position over and over again and for being my support every step of the way. The board of Headwaters was much more interested in my experience than in my age, and decided that I was a good fit for where they wanted to go as an organization. It feels so good to be somewhere that encourages me to be myself and where I get to stretch my skills every single day to make Minnesota a more just place to live and work.

I wrote this book with Rosetta because I think that young people have a lot to offer to the social sector and that the challenges that we face, nationally and globally, will take the expertise of all generations to solve.

How Do You Get from Here to There?

Our stories may sound like pure luck to you, but in reality, we both utilized many of the strategies we're about to share with you to advance our careers and move up the nonprofit career ladder much faster than the average young professional. What has been proven over and over to us is that you cannot wait for your organization to "develop" you. The most successful nonprofit careers are marked by a proactive approach to professional growth and leadership development. So, you don't have to wait for your boss or your supervisor to show you how to move up in your career. You *can* do this on your own, and we're here to help.

This book is divided into chapters on developing expertise, building a strong network, your personal brand, authentic leadership, balance, and moving up. Each chapter has a variety of tips that will help you grow in these areas. This book is designed for you to read from start to finish or read the chapters that interest you most first. Think of this as a cookbook for your career and try out the recipes that sound good to you.

Chapter 2: Develop Expertise

The most important part of building a great nonprofit career is being good at what you do. There is absolutely no way you can advance in your organization or within the field if you suck at your job. The following tips will help you find the right organization and become much better at your current job in order to help open up leadership opportunities for you in the future.

Tip 1: Find a Great Nonprofit Job

Nonprofit jobs can be a wonderful opportunity to live your values through your work, if you find something that is a good fit for your values and interests. Alfonso Wenker knew early on that he had a passion for social justice and nonprofit work. He started volunteering for various HIV/AIDS and lesbian, gay, bisexual, transgender (LGBT) nonprofits starting at age 16. During his junior year of college he was hired as a part-time program manager at PFund, a community foundation that provides grants and scholarships to LGBT communities. Alfonso primarily coordinated the grant and scholarship review processes. He continued to ask for more responsibility and learned about all aspects of the foundation's operations including fundraising, finance, and program design. He also attended numerous trainings, joined groups like Emerging Practitioners in Philanthropy and asked community leaders to do informational interviews.

He's now been on the job for three years. Just two years out of college, he's been promoted to director of programs. Alfonso has built a peer network in the sector that he credits with bringing him opportunities like serving on the Emerging Practitioners in Philanthropy-Minnesota steering committee; being appointed a co-chair of the 2011 National Conference on LGBT Equality: Creating Change; and launching a blog, From Our Perspective, on LGBT movements and nonprofit jobs as a vocation. Alfonso says that advancing in his career would not have been possible without open lines of communication with his boss, young professionals' networks, professional development opportunities, and a personal focus and mission regarding the type of work he wants to do.

The trick to finding a great nonprofit job is to:

Know yourself

What sort of work are you good at and what skills do you still want to learn to help you reach your long-term career goals? The ideal position would be a mix of those two things.

Do your research

Are there similar organizations? What sets this one apart? How do people talk about the organization? Too positive might mean that you are a cog in a well-functioning machine; too negative might mean that either the organization is a sinking ship or it just might be an opportunity for you to shine in a place that is seeking new ideas and leadership.

Notice the culture

Organizational culture is nothing more than the organization's personality. Just like you wouldn't marry someone without really understanding their personality, you shouldn't commit to a job without digging up some clues on the organizational culture. Here are some clues to look for:

- **Mission:** Is the mission clearly articulated? Does it feel like the staff who are interviewing you are connected to the mission themselves?

- **Management:** Is the organizational flat or are there many layers of hierarchy? How do people talk about the organization's leadership? Inspirational leader, data-driven manager, power-crazed lunatic?

- **Work Space:** Are there many closed offices, surrounded by administrative gatekeepers? If so, it might be tough to pitch your ideas to top leadership without a hall pass and three forms of identification. Is the office an open room filled with beat up tables and piles of files? If that's the case, you may not be getting the corner office that you have been dreaming about.

- **Staff Diversity:** When you walk through the office or see their staff in the community does there seem to be a diversity of backgrounds and personality types represented? Do the staff seem to be representative of the community being served? Are people of color or young people concentrated in one type of the position in the organization (i.e. administrative or outreach positions)?

- **Work Environment:** Do staff seem rushed or very leisurely? Does there seem to be some sense of work/life balance? Are titles important in the culture? Do people in the organization socialize outside of work?

Once you know what sort of organization you would like to work for, it becomes a different ball game in terms of positioning yourself for a place in that organization. You goal is to do what it takes to make yourself the inside candidate. If you are currently in school or not working, an internship or significant volunteer commitment might be your ticket in to the organization of your dreams. Volunteering for an organization gives you a unique window into the organization's culture and allows key decision makers to see you in action. If you fill a unique organizational need with your volunteer position, you may also be able to help the organization develop a permanent position filling that same role.

If you aren't able to volunteer for an organization that you are interested in, be sure to use your network to help turn you into the inside candidate. Talk to any contacts that you have that work at the organization to put in a good word for you and to help you get the name and contact information for the hiring manager. It is often much better to contact the hiring manager directly rather than going through HR.

Your first nonprofit job isn't a make-or-break decision for the rest of your career in the sector, but it can better position you for your future plans. A better fit with space to grow in expertise or in title is a great first step!

Are you geographically flexible?

If you can move for the right position, you may be able to get great experience at a different level of responsibility than is available in your current location. Moving across the state, across the country, or to the other side of the world may make you more marketable for future positions. Allison Jones, a young nonprofit leader who blogs at AllisonJ.org, has four criteria that she suggests looking at when considering the best cities for young nonprofit professionals.

1. **Size and scope of the nonprofit sector:** Employment statistics, usually available from the local council of nonprofits or United Way, can give you a picture of how large and sophisticated the local sector is and help you figure out if there is room for you to grow.

2. **Government/nonprofit partnerships:** Look for a city where nonprofits have a vocal presence and are viewed by local government officials as a partner in solving tough social problems.

3. **Rates of volunteerism:** A city with a culture of participation will often indicate a thriving nonprofit sector.

4. **Number of active young professionals groups:** Seek out cities where you will have a built-in network of support. Do Internet searches for organizations that match your interests and see if they have active local chapters - for example, Young Nonprofit Professionals Network (YNPN) chapters, Emerging Practitioners in Philanthropy (EPIP) chapters, leadership development

programs through the local chamber of commerce, or Social Venture Partners organizations.

Don't tell anyone... but sometimes nonprofit jobs really suck

Many people think just because you work for a good cause, your workplace will always be hunky-dory. You'll come into the office or program site in the morning and everyone will be smiling and jumping up and down with excitement about saving the world. And your boss and board members will all be swell people of the highest character. While these are all nice sentiments about nonprofit work culture, they're not always true. Nonprofit workplaces can be plagued with the same irritations as for-profit companies: office politics, incompetent bosses, lying, stealing, lazy co-workers, etc. But if you don't go into it with rose-colored glasses, you can avoid hating your nonprofit job. Take time to answer this question: What kind of work environment do you need to be satisfied and happy?

Here are some examples of factors that nonprofit professionals often overlook when searching for a new job.

Being in close quarters

Many nonprofit offices are so tiny you can hear everything – every strike on the computer keyboard, every phone call, every stomach growl. Working in cubicles is more common than having an office with a door. If you need privacy in your work environment, you should be sure not to take a job where you won't get any.

Working on evenings and weekends

Many nonprofits hold events at night or on the weekends as part of their programs or for fundraising purposes. If you don't want your nonprofit job to interfere with your after-work happy hours or weekend activities, you should find out what the nonprofit's culture is before you accept the position. Ask your potential employer what a typical week would look like, as well as what a "worst-case scenario" week might consist of as well.

No support for professional development

This is by far one of the biggest complaints by nonprofit professionals about their work environment. Many organizations don't have the budget to pay for additional training or staff development. On the other hand, there are also nonprofits that do have the funding to support professional development, but still don't give employees enough time off or a flexible work schedule to take advantage of available learning opportunities. Oftentimes, nonprofit workers have to pay for conferences and workshops out of their own pocket as well as use their vacation time to attend. Be your own best advocate in the job searching and benefits negotiation process to make sure you're joining an organization that will support your ongoing growth as a nonprofit professional.

If you don't do your due diligence on the type of nonprofit work environment you're signing up for, it's nobody's fault but yours. These items may at first seem like minor considerations, but if you plan to stay in a position for a while, they can wear on you. Choose your next nonprofit job carefully so you can love your work with a passion ... instead of hating it with a passion.

Tip 2: Size Matters

A common topic of nonprofit debate is "where is the best place to gain experience, the small or the large nonprofit?" The most unhelpful answer is "whatever feels best to you." The reason this is unhelpful advice is because if you are looking for your first nonprofit job or have only worked at small or large organizations you have nothing to compare it with. So here are some of the points to think about when considering a position at a small or large organization.

Small Organizations

The Good

A small organization means that you can be a big fish in a small pond. Small organizations (usually less than 10 staff members) need you to take a larger leadership role because the organization can't be successful if you aren't pulling your full weight. This means that, even as a new staff member, you could learn how to do things like budgeting, fundraising, volunteer management, and project planning. These generalist skills will serve you well throughout your career or will help you learn early on which skills you would like to develop more fully in a specialized position.

Megan Powers was a program manager at a nonprofit association group called Asian Americans/Pacific Islanders in Philanthropy (AAPIP). In her position, she worked in a team of four to develop methods for building the capacity of small nonprofit organizations in more responsive and culturally competent ways. Being part of such a small staff meant that she was responsible not only for management of the program – financial reports, fundraising, and drafting reports and evaluations – but that she was also able to develop her creativity and innovation by developing curriculum and facilitating technical assistance sessions.

After being at AAPIP for three years, Megan was recruited to take a position as Senior Project Manager at Grassroots Solutions, a consulting firm that found the combination of Megan's creative skills and managerial skills to be appealing for the firm's work. She now leads a team on a variety of projects around the country to help nonprofits, foundations, campaigns, and for-profit companies engage their constituencies more effectively.

Small organizations also have the ability to be very nimble, and if you can be flexible you will be rewarded with an exciting position where everything you do is critical to the success of the organization. Your work and the systems that you help create will benefit the organization for many years after you leave.

The Bad

If you are at a small organization, you can usually expect that there will not be a lot of money or time available for your own professional development. Conferences and trainings are a luxury that many small organizations can't afford. If you are working at a small nonprofit, you have to take the initiative to create your own professional development plan and you may also have to pay for some of the trainings on your own.

In small organizations, you also don't have a lot of back-up or support to do the tasks that you are working on. That can mean that a three-month maternity leave is followed by three months of work to do when you return because there are not enough staff members to pick up the slack. You might also get burned out by wearing so many hats. The large workload and varied responsibilities at a small nonprofit can spell disaster if you are unprepared for the stress.

Paul Nazareth, manager of planned and personal giving at the Catholic Archdiocese of Toronto, says, "At one time I was at a small charity as the sole fundraising officer. I had to do my own prospecting, planning, strategy, and most of all administration and paperwork." You can sometimes feel far away from the mission in a small organization because you are too busy to see the bigger picture.

The Ugly

Sometimes 'small' or 'start-up' can mean 'not fiscally sound.' In the worst-case scenario, you have to raise your paycheck to get one. This isn't always the case but it is something that you should always be aware of. If you do work for an organization that isn't financially stable, keep an updated resume and 3-6 months of living expenses in savings.

Maddy, who worked at a small nonprofit organization, felt like her world was crumbling around her when almost half of her very small staff left in a period of a few months because of budget pressures. "It was suddenly just me and my co-worker trying to make the budget. We didn't have the positional authority to make any of the decisions about the long-term future of the organization, but we were left holding the bag as those decisions were being made." The situation caused Maddy, who was a development director at the organization, to leave for a development officer position at a large, well-established organization. "There is a lot less pressure working for a large organization. I'm sure that my paycheck will clear when I put it in my bank account."

Big Organizations

The Good

Working at a large nonprofit gives you the opportunity to work a very specialized position in a large system. Because there are so many people in the organization, you can see many management and working styles and decide which types work best for you. Bigger organizations usually have better communications, marketing, and fundraising functions. Seeing how those functions operate will help you if you take a position at a smaller organization and you can bring those experiences with you.

Another benefit of really large organizations is that they may be connected to a larger network of national organizations (think the Girl Scouts or the Red Cross), connected to other similar organizations locally (think United Way networks), or could be so big that they have their own in-house training and professional development (you see this at many universities). Connecting with similar organizations gives you a forum to trade best practices and to build your professional network.

Aretha Green-Rupert was a Chief Development Officer at a local office of the Girl Scouts. In her position, she was able to connect with people in identical positions at Girl Scout Councils throughout the state and the country: "It was wonderful to be able to talk with peers who have the same challenges and were using the same messaging as our council. We would meet together at least once a year and bring all of our fundraising materials; as well as conduct content specific quarterly conference calls. I would often find materials and ideas that were perfect for our next campaign."

The Bad

For most people that join the nonprofit sector, they do so because they want to be close to the action. At a large organization, sometimes you are very far away from the work. It can be hard to be motivated by mission if you are three levels of staff away from the people being served.

The Ugly

Sometimes being at a big organization makes you feel like you are in the bowels of a ship rowing with 100 other people. It doesn't seem like it will make a big difference if you stop rowing, since you can't see where you are going and you are definitely not steering the ship. Ann Rosenfield, a fundraiser in Toronto says, "The access to professional resources is a huge plus at a big charity, but on the downside it can be like trying to move the Titanic to get change to happen. You can spend hours of your life getting approvals and forms filled in." Determining what aspects of your job give you a real sense of purpose and direction is important early on; otherwise you won't have the motivation that helps you do your best work.

Remember that one organization is probably not going to be the entirety of your nonprofit experience, so going to a large or small nonprofit does not need to be a make-or-break decision. Over your career if you have a good balance of big and small organizations, you'll develop leadership skills plus specialized knowledge ... a great combination!

Nonprofit Rockstar: Sabena Leake

Sabena Leake has effectively managed the balance between small and large nonprofits. After being a program officer for a family foundation, she realized that she had a special ability to act as a translator between small nonprofits and institutional funders. She left her philanthropy job and became a consultant for Tamar Consulting, where she helps small grassroots nonprofits develop their fundraising strategy.

"I was at a couple 'large' nonprofits, but decided to leave my position as Program Officer at the Andrus Family Fund because I felt like I was working too far from the

communities that I wanted to assist (namely black and Hispanic communities). The time to meet, lunch, conference, develop policies, conduct studies, write papers, etc., while sometimes necessary, are luxuries that folks in these communities don't often have.

So after many years of observing, learning, and developing my skills in these larger institutions - particularly of learning and observing how to leverage resources to get things done - I decided to move into the community where I apply these skills in a more practical way to make a more immediate difference."

Tip 3: Make the Most of Your Volunteer Experience

There is always a wonderfully rewarding feeling in giving your time and talents to a worthy cause. Feeding the homeless, tutoring children, or playing games with senior citizens can all give you a sense of community as well as help you grow as a person in the process. But many young professionals just stop at the warm fuzzy feeling they get from giving back instead of going the extra step taking on leadership roles as volunteers. We call this "volunteering for free." Why? Because you are probably overlooking all of the other opportunities in volunteering that can help you in your career. It's kind of like being a waiter that leaves the tip on the table. Especially if you're actively seeking a new nonprofit job, it's important that you use every chance you get to further your job search process. If you're going to volunteer, try to choose opportunities that allow you to build your resume, make new contacts, or learn a new skill.

Build your resume

If you choose a volunteer position that allows you to lead in some capacity, it looks a lot better on your resume than simply "volunteered to clean the local dog park." If your goal is to obtain a job in the environmental field, for instance, you want to show that you can play a leadership role in the organization if they decide to hire you. If you want to go ahead and clean up the dog park or the river, step up and be the organizer or rally other volunteers so you can state your accomplishments on your resume as "recruited 100 volunteers to clean the dog park, the largest turnout ever." Much more impressive, yes?

Make new contacts

True story: Rosetta once volunteered to staff the registration table at an event just so she could meet the organization's CEO and mingle with the staff so she could have a better chance of getting a job there. It was a great way to build relationships with the right people so that when her resume crossed their desk, they already would know who she was. You have the choice of volunteering at thousands of different nonprofits, but why not make it a win-win by helping out with one of the ones you may want to work for in the future?

Learn a new skill

No offense, but anyone can ladle soup into a bowl to feed the homeless. It's a worthy activity, but it won't do much for your career as a skill if a six-year-old could do it. If you're a nonprofit jobseeker, try your hand at helping out with something you don't already know how to do. If there's an organization that needs help putting up flyers for a new program or campaign, volunteer to be the one to design them even if you have no design experience whatsoever. It could force you to learn new software like Photoshop very quickly and you'll be able to add it to your resume in case your new job requires you to know something about design or print marketing.

Now don't get it twisted. We're not telling you to stop volunteering. We're just saying to use your volunteer time wisely. If you're going to give back, use your experience to kill two birds with one stone: help your community and help your career at the same time!

Nonprofit Rockstar: Lauren Mansene

Lauren is currently the communications coordinator for Sojourner Center, a Phoenix-based domestic violence program for women and children. She also serves as a board member and committee chair for the Lincoln Family Downtown YMCA in Phoenix.

In addition to her role at Sojourner Center, she is the chair of the PR committee for the YMCA's annual half marathon and 5K walk event. By serving another nonprofit in this fashion, she has been able to tap into connections she already has as well as grow her social capital through another group of individuals. By taking on a volunteer role in an organization that has a very different focus than her current job, she gets to tap into other skills that she doesn't normally use on a day-to-day basis.

Tip 4: Learn How to Raise Money

Fundraising is the lifeblood of any nonprofit organization. Knowing how to do this well puts you in the running for many senior level jobs, including: program director, development director or advancement director, and especially the executive director role. Even if you don't yet know diddly-squat about fundraising, there are lots of resources out there to help you learn, including one of our favorites, The Fund Raising School at The Center on Philanthropy at Indiana University. The only program of its kind, The Fund Raising School focuses on the art and science of fundraising and philanthropy. If you want to learn from the best, this would definitely be the place to do it!

In short, good fundraisers know how to:

Make the case

You can't serve a nonprofit well if you can't make the case for why the organization should receive support or why it should exist. Effective fundraisers are able to distill an organization down to its most essential elements and get people excited to help support the mission.

Design programs

Grantwriters are often the ones who can tell if a program will or will not be successful. If you are unable to describe the logic model of a program or how a program creates changes in the life of participants, it probably isn't a very successful program. Expertise writing grants and writing grant reports helps you learn to identify quality programming.

Keep asking

Fundraisers get a lot of no's. Learning how to accept those no's with grace, as well as learning how to turn a short-term no into a long-term yes are important skills that you can use in many settings.

Keep people informed

Organizations keep supporters and volunteers by keeping key stakeholders informed about what is happening in the organization. Good fundraisers are great communicators.

Write a budget

Creating a project or organizational budget helps you understand what it takes to make an organization operate. Fundraisers have to understand the budget, write the budget narrative explaining it, and creating the final budget will help you learn to navigate your organization's financial processes.

Write well

Staying within page guidelines and making a clear, compelling case through your writing is useful for aspects of your professional life. Writing a resume, summarizing your accomplishments for the year when you are asking for a raise, and even writing emails all will be more professional if you strengthen your writing skills.

Fundraising might also be a step on a different career path. As a graduate student, Trista had a mentor that encouraged her to become a fundraiser before going into a career in philanthropy. Dr. Bill Diaz was a former program director at the Ford Foundation but had also had a long career in the nonprofit sector. He said that, as a grantmaker, it was important to know what it feels like to sit on the other side of the table during a conversation about funding. He also suggested that she use those site visits to figure out which foundations she would like to work for. If a program officer treated her with respect and asked thoughtful questions, she could take that as a positive sign that they were well-trained and that the foundation had similar values about how nonprofits should be treated in the application process.

By the way ... you don't need to be a professional fundraiser to raise money

Anthony Colon is a Miami-based executive who knows how to have a good time. His house parties are the stuff of legends. A few years ago he decided to tie his entertainment expertise with his quest to make the world a better place. Through his "philanthroparties" he joins forces with nonprofit organizations ranging in areas of focus (environment, human rights, arts and culture, etc) to raise funds. Here's how it works:

Anthony calls two nonprofits and asks them if they are interested in participating in being "featured" at the party. A joint guest list is created and Anthony takes care of putting on the party. Guests are charged a suggested contribution. Information and literature is provided in "swag bags" to everyone that attends. Through creative installations and entertainment, everyone is introduced to the work of the featured organizations. Before everyone leaves, each person is asked to select the organization they would like to disburse their suggested contribution to. His friends are exposed to new organizations, are tied to an informal giving circle, and have a great time.

Anthony says, "My passion is donor organizing. These parties are a way to engage friends for whom charitable giving isn't something they necessarily think about. It's a fun way of getting people informed about how collectively small donations can amount to big change."

Think of what skills or interests that you have that could help a nonprofit raise funds and help you strengthen your fundraising skills. Could you:

- Volunteer to help with a capital campaign?
- Help plan an event?
- Host a house party?
- Call your friends and ask them to write a check for your favorite cause?
- Set up a social media fundraiser?
- Coordinate an eBay auction?
- Join a development committee?
- Write a grant for your favorite organization?

Fundraising for a cause that you care about will help you learn skills that will be useful throughout your career and will help those organizations meet their mission.

Tip 5: Always Learn, Always Teach

It is critical that you never stop aggressively learning your craft. The sector's needs change, techniques improve, and new thought leaders emerge everyday with ideas that will improve our quest to make the world a better place.

Here are some ideas of how you can always be learning:

Ask a lot of questions

Never be too cocky and think you have nothing more to learn about your position. Ask your co-workers if you can shadow them if they do similar work. Join a network of people with a similar position to learn how to do your job better.

Stay on top of the news

Blogs, nonprofit news sites, and other sector's news sources are great ways to stay on top of trends and current thinking about your field. Subscribe to sources that you find helpful and set aside time weekly or daily to check out those sites.

Gossip isn't always bad

Some of the best information about future trends or news about a specific organization comes through gossip. Don't spread info that you don't think is true but make some time for more informal conversations to stay in the know.

Get credentialed

Sometimes a more formal learning environment is what's needed to move your career to the next level. Talk to people in your field that have gotten a certification like the CFRE (Certified Fund Raising Executive) or a specific degree and figure out what makes sense for you in the long term.

While always learning is critical, remember that you are not some empty vessel that needs to be constantly filled by others. You have a lot of skills and expertise to share as well.

Here are some ways to teach:

Help new staff out

When a new staff member joins your organization, step up and be willing to teach them the organization culture, as well as where the office supplies are located. You'll make a new friend and an additional ally in the organization.

Be a mentor

College students, people new to your field, and sector-switchers are all people that may ask you for an informational interview or for a more formal mentorship relationship. Be open to people seeking new information. You'll increase your professional network, share some of your expertise, and learn a lot in the process.

Jessica Schaeppi moved to Minnesota from New York and was interested in building her network in a new state. She asked for an informational interview with Trista. During that meeting, Trista found out that Jessica had helped start a very successful giving circle in New York City that was very much like a circle that Trista wanted to build at the Headwaters Foundation. Jessica became an Advancement Fellow for Headwaters and helped the foundation build the groundwork for this giving circle.

Be a teacher

Host a lunchtime book club on topics of interest to your co-workers, you'll learn something new and position yourself as someone "in the know" in your organization. You may also want to teach in a more official capacity at a local university or professional program. Talk to others that have gone this route to see what the requirements for those positions are; it isn't nearly as tough as you think.

Position yourself as an expert

Being an expert just means that you have taken the time to learn more about a topic than other people in your field. Pick your expertise area and then be as knowledgeable as possible. Present at local conferences on this topic, write articles for professional journals, or start your own blog.

Nonprofit Rockstar: Marc Pitman

Marc A. Pitman has successfully branded himself as a fundraising expert. He is the author of "Ask without Fear!" and founder of FundraisingCoach.com, a website dedicated to practical ideas for fundraising more effectively. He also teaches internet marketing at Thomas College.

With successful experience fundraising for colleges, prep schools, and healthcare, Marc's enthusiasm for fundraising has caught the attention of such organizations as Reuters, the Canadian Broadcasting Corporation, the Chronicle of Philanthropy, and the American Marketing Association. His lively presentations at conferences and fundraising seminars get him invited to various organizations like Blackbaud's Conferences for Nonprofits, Habitat for Humanity International, the New England Association for Healthcare Philanthropy, and the Association of Fundraising Professionals.

"As fundraisers, we know asking questions is important. That goes for our professional development as well. Find people that are further down the road than you and ask them insightful questions.

"I did this with David Dunlop at my first development conference at Dartmouth College. Dave is a true guru, a person who's shaped professional development as a field. Yet no one was picking his brain during the breaks! I made it a point to ask him his opinion about whatever the previous seminar was. He graciously answered my questions and spent far more time with me than I would've expected. His passion for always involving volunteers and his proven track record of raising billions inspires me to this day.

"After that conference, I sought out time with him, even driving him to the airport on one occasion. Not only has that interaction molded me and shaped my career, it has opened doors with others who were also impacted by Dave. Those initial conversations sent my career, both as a fundraiser and as a fundraising trainer, on a trajectory I never would have imagined."

Tip 6: Work Abroad

When Allyson Reaves' grandmother, North Carolina matriarch that she is, strongly advised in her stern yet caring way that foreign languages would catapult Allyson's working existence to the next level, she had no idea that this curiosity for language, culture, and social richness would lead to a career in international philanthropy. Allyson is the current program manager for the Transatlantic Community Foundation Network in Canada, and here she shares a few ideas for those considering the international side of nonprofit work.

Speak openly about your goals

Allyson shared her goals about working internationally with colleagues and superiors, and with their support and encouragement she found some great opportunities. While she was working at the Community Foundation of the Lowcountry (South Carolina), her mentor and former supervisor slid her the application to participate in a three-month International Fellows Program at The Center on Philanthropy and Civil Society (The Graduate Center at CUNY). A few months later, she received the fellowship, and it was extremely pivotal in shaping her experiences.

Conduct research, get published, and distribute internationally

There are so many facets of building and managing knowledge in third sector work; and distributing research is a very manageable way to work internationally. Research gave her the platform to express her views and build her network. Each year, identifying a topic that is relevant to the field has enabled her to work in many different ways and with a wide scope of people and organizations.

Work outside the box (and outside the job!)

Sometimes the most opportune jobs aren't really jobs. Keep an eye out for consulting opportunities, fellowships and, internships that are hosted and funded by foundations, organizations, and government branches outside of the US. Allyson's yearlong work at Fondazione CRT (a banking foundation in Torino, Italy), was actually the Master dei Talenti program (a blend of professional work and an apprenticeship) which enabled international participants to work in various areas of social justice.

The nonprofit sector has many opportunities for practitioners to build cross-border work. The learning opportunities for countries, cultures, and traditions to grow from each other are numerous, and finding your space will add tremendous value to the mission and vision of global change.

Chapter 3: Build a Strong Network

You've heard this many times before: The key to getting your dream nonprofit job is to network, network, and network some more. You've heard it so many times because it's true. Even in the technology age, you simply cannot restrict your job search to online job boards and email. Back in the day, before Twitter, Facebook, and LinkedIn, nonprofit leaders actually made connections face to face most of the time. These days, technology has made communication much less time-consuming, but the old-fashioned ways of networking still hold true. Here are a few ways to build your network.

Tip 7: Prioritize Networking

Although the term "networking" can conjure up a bleak picture of a crowd of people trying to impress one another, young nonprofit professional Shannon Mouton aptly defines it this way:

Networking is meeting people to develop a mutually beneficial professional relationship.

Sounds good to us. Let's keep it real – we all know that when you're ready to take that next big leap in your career, it's really more about who you know than anything else. But if you're a nonprofit professional just starting out in your career, it can be a daunting process to put yourself out there when you don't know anyone. We recommend taking the time to attend at least one networking event per month and attend conferences to meet people both in and outside of your field. Pick a social network you like and connect with like-minded folk. We know the membership fees can be steep, but you can meet many great people (and potential mentors!) through professional associations.

Whatever you do, don't put networking on the back burner. Your network is your greatest tool when it comes to preparing for the next step in your career. Your network will help you identify positions, give you the courage to apply, and be your best inside and outside advocates to get you that position. Your network can also be a source of support for challenging situations or for advice and support about how to balance it all.

Tip 8: Attend Nonprofit Conferences

Nonprofit conferences are the mecca of networking. You get to learn from some of the top leaders in the field as well as build relationships with others in the sector. Of course, conference attendance can get a little pricey, but having the opportunity to meet hundreds of nonprofit professionals in one place is usually worth it. You will meet your peers, as well as experienced nonprofit leaders who could be your next boss.

Top-notch annual nonprofit conferences to attend include:

- Independent Sector Annual Conference
- Craigslist Nonprofit Boot Camp
- NTEN Nonprofit Technology Conference
- Council on Foundations Annual Conference
- Annual meetings held by your state nonprofit association

Make sure you meet people

Networking at a swanky nonprofit conference can sound like more fun than anything, but we urge you to be strategic about your networking time. You actually do yourself a real disservice when you attend an event without a purpose in mind. If you spend the time and money to go to a conference and then they go home without ever exchanging a single business card, you've wasted your time. Why go to an event in your industry and not connect with the very people who can help you further your career and vice versa? Remember, you don't need to meet everyone at the conference; just focus on a few people that are in your field or that you are interested in getting to know better. And please, whatever you do, don't forget your business cards!

Tip 9: Get Your Own Business Cards

This is one of the most important things you can do for your personal brand (especially for jobseekers). Ever since Rosetta was 18, she's had her own business cards. Even when she was working a full-time job, she kept a stack of business cards in her purse to let people know about her blog and where to contact her outside of her 9-to-5 nonprofit job. Our favorite place for business cards is Vistaprint. Rosetta has used them for the past 10 years because of their low cost, easy-to-use website, and quick delivery. And when we say low cost, we mean low cost. New customers get 250 premium quality, color business cards free. (You just pay for shipping.) They also have a ton of professional business card templates, but keep yours simple.

If you're just now making up a set of personal business cards, you may be wondering what you should include on them. Here are a few ideas that you can run with.

- Your name
- Your title, tagline, or motto (for example, you can use blogger, writer, consultant, or fundraising professional)
- Your blog address, if you have one
- Your email address
- Your phone number (if you want to give it out)
- Your social networks (if you want to give them out)

And don't be afraid to tell people how you want them to interact with you. For instance, the backside of Rosetta's business cards say "hire me" pretty prominently. People always comment on how bold it is. But you have to remember that marketing yourself is a lot like marketing a product. You have to tell people what action you want them to take after they see what you have to offer.

Tip 10: Join Professional Associations

Professional associations are great places to learn more about your field, flex your leadership muscles, and build your professional network. Membership fees can be expensive but sometimes your employer can pay for it or, if you are still in school, you can get a student rate. Here are some reasons to join a professional association:

Continuing education

Most professional associations have journals or newsletters that will keep you up-to-date on trends in your field. They also have conferences or other professional development opportunities where you can learn from the experts in your field.

Connection to other members

Membership lists of professional associations will give you great contacts in your field, whether you are looking for employment or a mentor. You will also be able to develop a larger network by serving on committees and attending networking events.

Job listings

Job boards are a great benefit of association membership. The specialized position postings mean that many more jobs are related to your area of interest than a traditional job board. It also looks good on your resume to list your membership in a professional association; it shows that you take your professional development seriously.

When segregation is good

There are many professional associations that are tied to your racial group, age, sexuality, or gender. Many nonprofit professionals wonder if this sort of self-segregating can be limiting. If you balance this sort of purposeful self-segregation with time spent with people that are very different than you, it can expand your horizons and make you a better professional. Trista explains:

"When I decided to go to a historically Black college, there were a variety of factors behind that decision. But the biggest factor was that I was sick of always trying to explain that racism really existed and I felt like I was spending too much time in high school being the 'black representative' on every topic. I developed a strong personal and educational footing at Howard because I wasn't spending all of my time dealing with the issues of race and privilege when I should have been studying for a stats test".

So what does this have to do with your nonprofit career? There are also times in your professional development that you have the choice of spending time with people that are like you in some way. Through affinity groups and your own professional networks, you decide what types of people you spend time with.

Trista has had amazing experiences with the Association of Black Foundation Executives, Emerging Practitioners in Philanthropy, and the Funding Exchange. She shares why she feels so connected to those networks and why some of her best thinking about her organization and her own professional development often happens after she has been spending concerted periods of time with peers from those groups:

1. **Diversity is important but it is also hard work.** Getting people to understand where you are coming from can take most of the conversation and then you might never get to talk about the action.

2. **You can go deep.** It is easier to do intensive work when you are with like-minded or like-experienced people that you don't have to tell that backstory to.

3. **Being with people with similar backgrounds and experiences can be a time of regeneration.** You can take down some of your barriers and think about who you are and what to bring to this work.

There is a time and place for spending time with people from backgrounds different than yours. Those experiences stretch your perspective and help you see new solutions to old problems. The point is to be purposeful and find times where you can spend some reflection time with people that have similar backgrounds.

Nonprofit Rockstar: Anthony Colon

Anthony Colon, who you may remember from the Learn to Raise Money tip earlier in the book, is executive director of the Green Family Foundation. The foundation is dedicated to supporting social programs that impact global health and alleviate poverty. Before joining the foundation, he served as senior program associate at the Funders' Network for Smart Growth and Livable Communities, a national network of philanthropic institutions focused on growth and development issues. He is a member of Emerging Practitioners in Philanthropy, Hispanics in Philanthropy, and has been involved in various programs of Resource Generation. He also has a master's in Public Policy Administration.

"I credit many of my professional relationships to affinity groups. The ability to connect with colleagues at conferences and through conference calls helps to tackle the isolation that can come from doing this type of work. Through my involvement with networks of Emerging Practitioners in Philanthropy, I was able to find others around the country who were working at foundations, that I could share struggles and strategies with. As my career has evolved, I have been able to develop a roster of 'contemporaries' that I can tap into both professionally and personally. It helps to be able to pick up the phone and call another 'young' executive director at a foundation that can understand the unique elements of this job."

Tip 11: Go Talk to People

So you're ready to move to a new position and have been combing all of the job boards. Then you hear that your colleague got a fabulous position at the local community foundation that you would love to work for. You didn't even see the position posted. What is going on? Welcome to the "hidden" nonprofit job market. According to a study by BH Careers International, 80 percent of all available jobs are never advertised. So how do you access this secret society? You expand your professional network to include people from the types of organizations that you would like to work for. The best way to strengthen your candidacy for a position is to have someone on the inside advocating for you.

The most effective way to meet potential advocates is through informational interviews. An informational interview means that you are seeking advice, rather than interviewing for a specific job. Here's how to make informational interviews work for you:

Set up meetings with people in the field you are interested in

Go through your contacts and set up your first informational interviews with people that you know. They are less intimidating and can provide referrals to other people from their networks that you can meet with. Another strategy is to come up with your stretch list of whom you would like to meet with. These are people that are well respected, local and national leaders that are either in your dream position or would be hiring for your dream position. Keeping track of when people from out of state are in your town to speak or attend a conference exponentially increases your chances to meet with them face to face. It is completely acceptable to contact someone out of the blue and ask for an informational interview or you could ask a mutual friend to introduce you.

Be clear

When you are setting up informational interviews, let the interview subjects know who you are and what you would like to learn from them. Have three questions available and give those to the person beforehand. Some examples:

- I'd like to move into your sector and have heard that you are well connected. Can you refer me to 2-3 other people?

- I want to work for an organization like yours someday. What do you look for when you are hiring?

- I am thinking about a specific graduate school program. Do you think this type of program would be useful for your type of work?

The person you are meeting with is not a mind reader. Tell them exactly what you are looking for and there is less of a chance of you being disappointed. Be prepared to get everything you need in 30 minutes and count any extra time as a gift.

Bring your "A" game

Treat informational interviews much like you would a regular interview. Arrive on time, dress professionally, bring something to take notes with, treat any administrative staff that set up the meeting or bring you to your interview subject with respect, and end on time. Most of your time in the meeting should be spent listening and asking follow-up questions. You are meeting with this person to learn what they know about the field or the organization, so don't waste this opportunity by talking too much.

You might be asking, "I thought I was setting up these interviews so I could get a job. How am I going to get a job if I don't tell the person that I am meeting with all of the wonderful qualities that I possess?" Thoughtful questions and the ability to listen and take advice are great qualities that many employers are looking for. If you turn this meeting into an infomercial for yourself, many people will be turned off and won't be as willing to help you in your job search.

Follow up appropriately

At the end of the meeting, be clear what you would like from the interview subject. For example, "Because I enjoy grantwriting, I'm planning to move into the fundraising field. If you hear of any positions where my experience would make me a good fit, please let me know." Another example is, "I'm looking to move into a management position in a mentoring organization. Could you suggest 2-3 other people that you respect who would be able to give me their perspective on managing this type of organization?"

Send the interview subject a handwritten thank-you note immediately after you meet. A thank-you email is better than nothing, but you are trying to make an impression here, so put the pen to paper. A great way to stay in contact in the long run is by sending articles or other information that you think would be useful for the people you have met with. It helps to keep you on their radar and lets them know that you are staying up-to-date about a field that they care about, too.

When you do find your dream position, make sure that you send another thank-you letter to all of the people that sat down with you as you were looking. Making people feel personally responsible for your success is a great way to show gratitude and to keep them invested in your further development.

There are lots of ways to conduct informational interviews. Here are some suggestions:

Meet in-person at their office

The benefit of doing interviews this way is that you get to see what their office is like. Seeing an office can give you an idea of organizational culture and in some cases can give you some idea of organizational salaries. Trista visited one foundation and the staff members had beautifully decorated offices with expensive furniture. Then, she visited another foundation where they had small cramped cubes piled with paper. Further research confirmed that the pay rates at the first foundation were about double those at the second one.

Meet at conferences

Conferences are a great way to meet many people from around the country in a short period of time. After the participant list for the conference is released, start scheduling your informational interviews. Some successful strategies to get on someone's jam-packed conference schedule is to schedule a quick morning coffee, a happy hour off-site, or a meal in an interesting place away from the conference hotel. Some networking experts use hobbies like running or kayaking as an "in" when scheduling informational interviews. If you know that the interview subject has a similar interest (make sure you take a look at their bio), doing a fun off-site activity will help you make a great first impression and give you plenty of time to learn about this person or their organization. Plus, you'll have a great time!

Use social media

LinkedIn, Facebook, and Twitter are great ways to reach out and ask short specific questions that you would usually ask in an informational interview. A recent query on LinkedIn was, "What is better preparation for managing a nonprofit, a masters of Public Policy degree or a masters in Business Administration?" Make sure that you use discretion when using social media; if you don't want your boss to know that you are asking the question, don't ask it online.

Host a party

Hosting a dinner party lets you get to know people on a more personal level. Rudy Guglielmo, a philanthropic consultant, and Sarah Hernandez, a foundation program officer, host annual theme parties with other social sector colleagues. Their last party was a celebration of Saint Martin de Porres, the Patron Saint of Hairdressers (imagine a party with lots of good food, conversation, and fake hair).

Have a good mix of people you know and people you want to get to know better. As you are mingling with your guests, you may have the opportunity to ask some of the questions that you might ask in a more traditional informational interview. These sorts of events expand your professional network and can be a lot of fun.

While informational interviews can be a great way to get advice and expand your network, remember that some people are jerks. That doesn't change just because you are having an informational interview with them. They either won't meet with you or will give you very depressing advice like, "You really don't have a chance of breaking into the foundation field, so don't get your hopes up." Thank them for their time and move on to someone who is more receptive and supportive.

Tip 12: Build Your Own Frankenmentor

In 2007, Trista had a great professional network that she could rely on for advice and connections but felt like she was really missing the emotional support that she needed to move on to the next phase of her career. She had great friends, but they didn't really want to talk about work stuff. She had coffee with a colleague who was expressing the same frustration, so they decided to start an informal coaching group of young female professionals who were ready to move to the next phase of leadership and would benefit from a community of support.

They called their group the "Fab 5." The five women were from academia, philanthropy, social enterprise, and business. Their titles included foundation executive director, leadership center director, national program manager for a Hispanic grantmaking program, in-house attorney for an environmentally-friendly concert promoter, and regulatory affairs attorney for a Fortune 500 law firm. Their diversity of experiences and perspectives led to rich conversations and new connections during their monthly meetings. Each meeting was hosted by one of the members on a rotating basis and included a time for check-in around a guiding question like "how to balance work and home," "finding volunteer opportunities that sustain you," or "managing up." Trista considers each of these women an important mentor in her life.

The model of group mentorship that was just described was not what you have been promised your whole life. You were promised that there would be one fairy godmentor that would magically find you right after college and would provide you with advice, encouragement, and maybe even chocolate cookies as she gave you all the tools you would need to be successful in your chosen career. She would be well connected and with just one phone call could get you an interview for the position that you have been dreaming of.

We're sorry to be the ones telling you that this is a fairy tale, but you'll be better off if you stop looking for this magical creature. Please don't continue sitting around waiting for your fairy godmentor. You have to be proactive and build your own Frankenmentor.

Your Frankenmentor will consist of all the best pieces of many people. It doesn't come in the pretty package that a fairy godmentor would, but you will get exactly what you need. The best Frankenmentors can provide you with emotional support, important connections to people, ideas, and resources, and advice on specific issues that you are facing right now. Many of the people that make up your Frankenmentor might not even see themselves as your mentor, but they are still able to give you what you need.

The three types of needs that you will have to fill with your collection of mentors are emotional support, topic-specific advice, and connections.

Build emotional support

It's important to have mentors that can provide you with emotional support so you don't quit in a hail of profanity and thrown papers. Remember to set up lunches and fun activities with other professionals that you want to deepen relationships with. If you are looking for more intensive emotional support, the Fab 5 structure might be for you. Here are a few more tips to get you started if you want to build your own Fab 5:

Purposeful recruitment

Diversity in fields, life experience, marital status, and race was important for Trista's group. The consistent factor of the Fab 5 was that they were all young women that were career driven and civically active. Decide on your own important consistent factors and areas where diversity would be critical.

Develop ground rules early

The original Fab 5's rules were confidentiality, equal speaking time, and rotating hosting responsibility.

Make the meetings consistent

Holding the meetings the same day of the month at the same time builds consistency and makes it more likely that people will make time in their schedule to regularly attend.

Limit the time

Trista's group agree that they would initially last for one year. It gives people time to re-evaluate if the group still is a fit for them and a time to leave gracefully.

Also remember that the best way to get emotional support is to give emotional support. Be available when people in your network are having a tough time at work or are in a career transition.

Topic-specific advice

Topic-specific mentors are experts in your field. They probably don't have time to be your full-time mentor, but they are great sources of advice when you have a specific question. Sherece West, the CEO of the Winfred Rockefeller Foundation, is that person for Trista. When the 35W bridge collapsed in Minnesota, killing 14 people and injuring 145, there was an outpouring of donations to help the victims. At the time, Trista was the Saint Paul Foundation's representative for the Minnesota Helps Bridge Disaster Fund. Sherece had been the CEO of the Louisiana Disaster Recovery Foundation after Hurricane Katrina and was a wonderful source of advice for Trista on how to manage the emotional toll of disaster grantmaking as well as the technical aspects of managing complex and time-limited grantmaking.

Build relationships with connectors

Connectors can be insiders in your industry who always seem to know what is going on, or they can be people from a completely different sector who are able to help connect you to people and resources that aren't available within your current network. Connectors are important because they usually know the missing piece when you are moving from point A to point B.

Lars Leafblad is a great example of a super connector. He is a principal with executive search firm Keystone Search and has built his business on knowing who the go-to people are on almost any topic. Many people in his network meet with him regularly to share information about new people that he should get to know and to expand their own networks. He has taken his super networking skills to a new level with his newsletter Pollen (available at www.MinnPost.com), which lists the recent accomplishments of people in his network, highlights new members, and links to interesting articles on social entrepreneurism, leadership, and other trends. And because Lars is such a wonderful networker, he's asked us to include a link to his LinkedIn profile so you can add him to your network (www.linkedin.com/in/larsleafblad)!

With a person like Lars in your network, you are just one or two degrees away from people who can give you advice on any topic or information on any organization.

Imaginary friends are not just for kids

In an ideal world you would have access to the best and brightest people in the world to give you advice and to tell you leadership parables over a cup of coffee. But maybe you live in Montana and your mentor of choice lives in Miami, or maybe your ideal mentor is too busy running the Children's Defense Fund to answer your question about writing a good research report. That doesn't mean that you can't benefit from their expertise.

Trista's learned the most about developing a solid career path from watching people that don't know her at all. She examines how they brand themselves, the positions that they have taken, the things they write about, and how they treat people – all important life lessons for her own career. Some of her current imaginary mentors include:

Marian Wright Edelman, CEO of the Children's Defense Fund

She is an amazing communicator and is able to bring the issues that she is passionate about to life for a very broad audience.

Susan Barresford, former CEO of the Ford Foundation

She worked her way through the ranks of the Ford Foundation to the top spot and created a culture of social justice philanthropy that was able to address root causes of societal ills.

Claire Huxtable, fictional mother on *The Cosby Show*

She is a great example of how to balance a successful career with a thriving and happy home life. The shots of her snuggled in the bed with Cliff while reading a court brief, give hope that you can bring home the bacon *and* fry it up in the pan.

Tip 13: Start Your Own Network

While it's wonderful to join an existing professional association, what do you do if that network doesn't exist in your community? Well, start your own, of course. Starting a professional network doesn't have to be nearly as complicated as it seems and the result will benefit you and your peers for years to come.

Every one of the professional associations that you hear about in this book, Emerging Practitioners in Philanthropy, the Young Nonprofit Professionals Network, or the Association for Black Foundation Executives started when one person or a group of people decided that they would be better off if they worked together to build their professional skills.

Rusty Stahl, the Founder and Executive Director of EPIP, shares the following story:

"I was working at the Ford Foundation as a program associate, and at that year's Council of Foundation's conference I happened to re-connect with a few young people working at foundations. We decided it would be fun to hold a dinner and try to create a space for young people attending the conference. So we handed out a bunch of flyers and were shocked when forty people showed up for dinner! When I got back to New York I was all excited about doing something to build on that gathering and, with the blessing of the folks at Ford, I began to work on developing what became known as Emerging Practitioners in Philanthropy. We now have chapters across the country and our network now includes more than 1,000 young foundation professionals, trustees, and graduate students studying philanthropy."

You don't have to start a nationwide network — you could start a local chapter of an existing network. Starting a local chapter just takes enthusiasm, some time, and a commitment to connecting with your peers. Most national organizations will give you technical assistance to help get the effort off of the ground.

Kristen Jeffers is getting the YNPN Triad Chapter off of the ground in Charlotte, North Carolina. She recalls:

"I was in DC at the Idealist Career Fair and saw information about the DC YNPN chapter. I thought YNPN could be an important resource in my community. Starting a chapter has been easy because of the support of many other young professional and civic organizations in the community. We coordinate our efforts. Through my work with the chapter I've strengthened my fundraising skills and have been able to use my marketing skills to increase local awareness of the chapter."

You may not have the title, but starting and leading your own network — especially one that reaches a large number of people — will help you develop the skills that you need to be a good executive director. By getting your own network off of the ground you learn how to set a strategic direction, motivate volunteers, mobilize resources, develop programming, and pull together a great team.

Chapter 4: Establish a Great Personal Brand

The nonprofit field is getting more competitive for top jobs as more and more candidates apply for positions with impressive education and experience. Instead of spending a fortune to go back to school, nonprofit professionals can make themselves stand out by developing a strong personal brand that potential employers can connect with.

But what exactly is a personal brand, you ask? Business management guru Tom Peters coined the term in 1997 with a fantastic manifesto titled "The Brand Called You" and this bold statement: "Big companies understand the importance of brands. Today, in the Age of the Individual, you have to be your own brand."

Another term for personal branding is "impression management," which comes from the field of leadership studies. Leadership scholar Gary Yukl defines impression management as "the process of influencing how others perceive you." Makes sense, right? But here's something even simpler: Your personal brand is essentially your professional reputation.

Let's face it. Everyone has a personal brand, whether you like it or not. It's what other people say about you when you're not in the room. It's what your references say about you when you apply for a job. So even when you ask someone to act as a reference for you, they do a quick gut check for how they feel about your personal brand. They decide whether they want to be aligned with your name and what you stand for, because their reputation is on the line too.

So, the question is not whether you have a personal brand or not. The real question is whether your personal brand a good one. What do people in your professional circle think of you? Do people even know who you are? Here are a few ways to get ahead of the personal branding game and position yourself for your next nonprofit career opportunity.

Tip 14: Google Yourself

"Regardless of age, regardless of position, regardless of the business we happen to be in, all of us need to understand the importance of branding. We are CEOs of our own companies: Me Incorporated. To be in business today, our most important job is to be head marketer for the brand called You." – Tom Peters

Yes, You Are a Brand

Just as certain thoughts pop into people's heads when they think of "iPod" (1,000 songs in your pocket) or "Subway" (Eat Fresh), when people think of you, as a professional, they should think of your personal "brand." Can you, a person have a brand? Of course! What do you think of when you think of Michael Jordan? Great basketball player, good jump shot, cool shoes, etc. What do you think comes to mind when people think about you? If you don't know, it is time to find out.

The Google factor

Are employers Googling you? Assume that they are. And if they can't find you, you pretty much don't exist. These days before anyone meets anyone, they run straight to Google to check out their web presence. Managing your presence on the web is one of the most important ways to manage your brand. To begin managing your web presence, Google yourself and analyze the following clues for what you may find.

Be visible

When searched, your name should appear somewhere on the first page of results. Have a common name? One way to make ensure that you stand out is to create several social media profiles for yourself with your photo to distinguish your brand from the others with the same name as you.

Be professional

Posts that mention you should be related to professional work, not embarrassing photos from college parties. If there is nothing professional about you online, create something!

Be relevant

Topics that should appear in search results include articles written, previous media interviews, references to jobs and internships, and professional networking affiliations. Remove content that is unrelated to work if you can. If removal is contingent on help from others, respectfully request that they remove content.

Be proactive

To push less relevant content below the first page, create newer, more relevant content and focus on moving it up in search results. You can enhance your online identity beyond high school newsletters and college sports score reports by doing a pre-emptive strike. Join online forums in your area of expertise and contribute regularly or start a professional blog.

How to monitor your online reputation

Depending on how active you are online, you may or may not be concerned about your online presence taking a downward spiral. If you post on many forums, blogs, etc. you might want to consider these helpful tracking tools that alert you when something new is posted about you.

- **Google Alerts**

  This is a free tool from Google that you can customize to scour various online services to find postings about you. You can configure Google Alerts so that it categorizes messages for easy reading. You can save or delete messages after you read them. Pro: It's free.

Con: It may not be as thorough as other tracking software.

- **Trackur**

  A fee-based tracking system that is highly customizable, Trackur allows you to set up searches based on keywords and keyword combinations. Your searches can be delivered to you via email or RSS feed. Pro: It's extremely thorough, customizable, and flexible. Con: You have to pay for the service.

- **Monitor This**

  Twenty-two search engines are searched by this software. Pro: It uses a comprehensive list of search engines. Con: You must know a bit about coding to make it work best for you.

- **Naymz**

  Similar to Trackur, though less expensive, a great feature of Naymz is that it allows you to keep track of all of your different web presences and monitor their content in an easy manner. Pro: If your reputation is being trashed, Naymz offers a "cleanup service." Con: It's fee-based, but less expensive and more comprehensive than some other fee-based programs.

Tip 15: Stop Trying to be Two Different People

Nonprofit professionals frequently express frustration at trying to keep their personal and professional identities separate. One evening at a networking event, Rosetta met a young woman who said that she wished she could bring the same social networking skills she uses with her friends online on Facebook to her professional networks. However, she felt that her work-related colleagues might judge her harshly for the personality traits she shares online. Rosetta pointed out that she could find a happy medium where she could be her whole self online and off, encouraging her to stop trying to be two different people. In the long run, it makes personal branding a lot easier. Here's why.

There is only one you

Really. You're just one person. There is no "personal" you and a "professional" you. Sometimes you're at work, and sometimes you're with your friends or family, but in both instances you're the same person. So why do we act as if we have multiple personalities? The best nonprofit leaders are the ones that can connect with others on as many levels as possible. It's okay to let people know that you're more than what you do at work, because you are. You may be a program director at your nonprofit, but you might also serve at your church or coach your child's basketball team. These details about your whole self are what make you interesting as a person, and allows others to find commonalities with you. Once you stop pretending as if you don't have a life before 9 and after 5, you'll be surprised at how many people will become drawn to you.

Remember that online, nothing is really done in the dark

As Rosetta's grandmother is fond of saying, "what's done in the dark will come to the light." Well, contrary to what you may think, nothing online is done in the dark. In fact, everything is done in the light because everything can be shared. Everything. If you send a private message to your friend on Facebook badmouthing someone, that communication can be forwarded, emailed, or posted up on a blog somewhere. If you use foul language or express any type of opinions on Twitter, those can be Googled and found as well. Therefore, you should strive to represent yourself in the best light possible no matter what part of yourself you're engaging.

Find a balance between personal and professional

It can be daunting trying to decide what to share and what not to share online and off. A good rule Rosetta has used is that she never shares anything she wouldn't mind showing up on the front page of the Washington Post. Now, her privacy bar might be set a little differently than yours, but figure out the line that works for you. Once, she tweeted about her breakup with a boyfriend and some of the insights she learned from the experience. If anything, it's helped Rosetta to appear more human to the people she engages as friends and colleagues. People feel like they know her better.

You never know how your social networks can help you

Rosetta has over 400 fans on Facebook, 500 contacts on LinkedIn, and over 9,000 followers on Twitter. She tends to update her social networks several times a day, sharing what she's working on, what she's writing about on her blog, what music she's listening to, or what she's doing for fun. She also shares articles she's reading (and her opinions on them) and blogs she recommends. Because she shares bits and pieces of her professional knowledge as well as what's going on with all of her other interests, the result is that many people see her not just as someone who knows a lot about nonprofits, but someone they like. To Rosetta's social networks, she's someone they feel they know enough to hire for projects or recommend to their networks. That is what you want your personal brand to do for you. You never know when an opportunity will come along just because you shared bits of your life online or off. For example, Rosetta has received most of her speaking invitations in the past year through her social networks. In fact, her first paid consulting gig came about because someone she knew online recommended her to their colleague offline. That probably wouldn't have happened if she was known for throwing f-bombs all over Facebook, but you get the point.

Tip 16: Write a Kick-butt Bio

"A bio is not so much factual as aspirational, and I feel compelled to put an aspirational paragraph in my own bio. Otherwise, how can I advise other people on setting goals for themselves that are a bit of a reach?" - Penelope Trunk, author of *The Brazen Careerist*

The main goals of a bio are to give the reader a clear sense of who you are and what you do, to establish your credibility, and to qualify your experience and background. If you can do all of these things, your bio becomes a distilled version of your personal brand.

Keep it short

When someone asks for your bio, they are not actually asking for your biography. Usually it is about a paragraph long and it is a story version of your resume. For longer versions of your bio, break the information into short, easier-to-read paragraphs. If your bio is too long, people won't read it, no matter how interesting you may be.

Refer to yourself in the third person

Normally this makes you look like an egotistical maniac, but it's a universal element of bio writing. Using the third person makes your bio look more professional and makes people more willing to trust what is in the bio.

Give 'em the good stuff

You want to demonstrate your professional credibility with your bio, so you don't need to list everything that is in your resume. Cover the high points of your career and remember nobody cares that you were a cashier at Target unless you are now the CEO of Target.

Tailor your bio to the audience

There are many different places you will use your bio, so make sure that you have different version for different audiences. You may need a bio for when someone is introducing you before you speak, a version for your organization's website, another version for your blog, a shorter bio for your LinkedIn profile, and an even shorter one for your Twitter profile. With each of these, think about the key pieces of information that each of these audiences needs to know about you.

Be yourself

Make sure that your bio reflects the real you. It's okay to use humor and you can also include information about your hobbies, family, and pets. It humanizes you. For instance, Dr. Emmett Carson, the CEO of the Silicon Valley Community Foundation, shares in his bio that he is *"married to Jacqueline Copeland-Carson, Ph.D. together they have the privilege, pleasure and occasional challenge of raising a teenage daughter."*

What's your hook?

You should include one or two pieces of information that will make your bio stand out. That makes it more likely that readers will remember this fact about you the next time you meet. Lars Leafblad, an executive search consultant, shares that he spent two summers in college competing in BBQ competitions across the upper Midwest as a member of the Famous Dave's of America National Touring BBQ Team.

A picture is worth a thousand words

Spend money on a headshot if you speak at conferences often or need to provide a picture for your organization's website. It gives you professional credibility and, if you are providing the shots yourself, you can set the tone. Rosetta's headshot has a tree in the background to emphasize her down-to-earth nature and Trista's has a solar panel in the background to be a visible example of her organization's commitment to environmental issues.

Tip 17: Professionalize Your Online Presence

With more and more nonprofit employers using social media to recruit and vet job candidates, it's increasingly important to control your online persona. By using the latest social media tools, you can ensure that you're putting your best foot forward online, as well as building professional relationships along the way. Revamping your presence on high-traffic social media sites like LinkedIn and Facebook is an easy way to professionalize your online presence.

Post Your Resume on LinkedIn

LinkedIn is THE place to make purely professional connections with your colleagues in the nonprofit field or even that great speaker you met at a conference. Sign up on www.linkedin.com and fill out a profile with your work experience and educational background. List your accomplishments and professional memberships. LinkedIn also allows other people to post recommendations of your work. There's no better way to market yourself than having someone else write a paragraph about how awesome you are!

For examples, you can view Rosetta's LinkedIn profile at http://www.linkedin.com/in/rosettathurman and Trista's at http://www.linkedin.com/in/tristaharris.

Professionalize Your Facebook Page

We know you originally created your Facebook profile to keep up with your friends in college. But you've graduated now, and guess what? Your Facebook profile can be Googled. So make sure you remove all of those photos of you doing shots at the bar. All of them. (I know, it was fun. But it's time to let go of the memories. Or at least just get rid of the evidence!) We're not saying not to be yourself, we're just encouraging you to consider whether your future employer would want to know about *that* side of you. Fill in the "Info" section of your Facebook page listing your previous jobs and educational background. And upload a nice headshot of your smiling face that anyone would love to hire. Don't forget those privacy settings.

Nonprofit Rockstar: Elisa Ortiz

Elisa Ortiz is currently the State Campaigns Director at Smart Growth America and attributes Twitter as a huge factor in advancing her nonprofit career. It has helped her to build a knowledge base on nonprofit best practices, resources, and technology which in turn, has allowed her to contribute intelligently to conversations within the office and provide evidence to back up her statements. In the last couple of places she's worked, she's also been one of the first people to find out about late breaking news or important new resources that have just come out relevant to our work. Both of these things have helped her build her 'clout' within the office and made her a more indispensable employee.

During her latest job search, Twitter definitely helped Elisa get noticed. Elisa says, "I was asked about my Twitter feed during a job interview and asked to provide some opinions on the use of social media within nonprofits. Being able to demonstrate a level of experience and knowledge helped me land that job."

Twitter has also allowed Elisa to develop some good relationships with nonprofit movers and shakers on Twitter. Those relationships have come in handy when she's needed support and they will again in the future.

Tip 18: Start a Blog

No one knew who Rosetta was until she started a blog. Seriously. She was a nobody. Even people who knew her from working with her at her organization didn't really "see" her until they saw her thoughts being posted online. She was a Director of Development for a reputable nonprofit with a master's degree, yet many people mistook her for her boss' secretary. When she would attend events hosted by her organization, people would ask her how long she had been an intern. How irritating!

One of the biggest benefits to having a blog is that even if you're not a big-shot CEO of your company, blogging can allow you to become well-known in your field. And the best thing you can do for your nonprofit career is to make sure lots of people know who you are. That way, when a juicy job opportunity or leadership role comes open, a bunch of people will be thinking of you as the perfect fit. That's exactly what happened for Trista.

Trista was a program officer at a local community foundation. It would have been very easy for her to do her work in relative obscurity. She started her blog, New Voices of Philanthropy, to chronicle the generational changes in leadership that she was seeing in the field of philanthropy. Through the blog she was able to develop her own voice and started to speak around the country about trends in philanthropy and the generational transfer of leadership.

When the Executive Director position became open at the Headwaters Foundation for Justice, she was able to show her experience as a spokesperson and the board was able to see how she articulated her viewpoints by reading the blog. Trista says, "As an executive director or president of an organization, your brand needs to match or complement the organization's brand because you are its most visible spokesperson. The board at Headwaters was able to look at my blog and know that my values and beliefs were a great match for the organization. I think my blog was my best reference when I applied for this position."

So, should you start a blog? Yes, if you want to use it to build your personal brand. No, if you just want to use it to complain about your life and only talk about personal issues that will not show off your expertise in your field. Stick to MySpace or Facebook for that. Also, don't start a blog if you're not going to have an opinion on anything! People will read you because they want to get information, but also because they want to know what you think. We're so tired of reading vanilla blogs that sound like all the posts came from a press release.

Putting your ideas out there on the big ol' Internet is scary for many young nonprofit professionals, but if you have something to say, it's a great way to get your voice out there. And people will respect you for it. Ask any blogger, and they will tell you that your reputation as a leader will soar once people see that you aren't hesitant to say what needs to be said. Once people (your readers) start to validate you, then others will start listening as well. No matter what age you are, people respect an expert. Starting a blog is the very best thing both of us have ever done for our careers. Blogging has led to consulting opportunities, speaking engagements, and much greater recognition for our work. Start simple by blogging about your passion for social change, and you never know what will happen.

Where to start

Google loves blogs. Google loves blogs so much, they have a special blog search. If you have a blog with your real name listed on it, Google will find it. Sign up at Blogger or Wordpress to get a free blog set up and start writing about issues that you care about, preferably somewhat related to the nonprofit field. It showcases your writing skills, social media savvy, and utter brilliance to future employers.

Get your own, self-hosted domain

Both Rosetta and Trista started with blogs on Blogger. There were simple templates to use and the focus could just be on content. As their online reputation grew and they got more savvy, both moved to self-hosted domains at WordPress. If we had it to do over again, we would have had our own domain from the beginning because having a .com instead of a blogspot.com or wordpress.com at the end of your blog address makes it easier for readers to find you. You should also think about using your full name as your domain name (i.e. RosettaThurman.com and TristaHarris.org). It makes it easier for people to find your blog and your content can change and grow over time without you changing your domain.

Blog under your real name

Rosetta thought about blogging anonymously at first, especially after writing a post in 2007 titled "Philanthropy Doesn't Care About Black People" on the Stanford Social Innovation Review blog, which created a firestorm of comments and emails that were quite overwhelming to her at the time. But being anonymous would have defeated the entire purpose of blogging for personal branding. If no one knew who was writing the articles, Rosetta would have reaped absolutely no benefit to her professional reputation. Plus, she had to learn how to stand up for her ideas no matter what people said about her. That's part of being a leader. It remains the greatest leadership experience that Rosetta has had through her blog.

Don't worry about your employer

When Trista first started blogging, she was worried that her organization would disapprove. After a piece that Trista wrote was picked up by the Chronicle of Philanthropy (where she said foundation staff weren't as pretty, funny, or as smart as they think that they are), she needed to have a long conversation with her foundation's communications director. The agreement they came to was that she would not list the organization's name in the blog and she wouldn't say anything that she wasn't comfortable saying in front of the foundation's board. For the record, she actually would have said that foundation staff wasn't as pretty, funny, or as smart as they think that they are in front of her organization's board. The organization was supportive of her blogging, but didn't see it as something that would improve the foundation's reputation.

Rosetta had a different experience. When Rosetta's boss saw her blog mentioned in the Chronicle of Philanthropy, he was thrilled. And when an article with her picture came out in the print version, he sent a note to all of the organization's members as well as the board. Her reputation in the nonprofit field made it easier for Rosetta to get several raises and the opportunity to travel around the country for professional development opportunities. Her organization was more willing to pay for them, not only because they wanted to keep her happy as an employee, but also because they perceived that she was worth it.

Know your organization and know how you using your own voice can be a benefit to its mission.

Visit these resources to help you figure out all the ins and outs of blogging:

- WeAreMedia blogging toolbox- www.wearemedia.org/Tool+Box+Blogs

- Problogger- www.problogger.com

- Copyblogger- www.copyblogger.com

- Blogging for Branding- www.bloggingforbranding.com

Nonprofit Rockstar: Jessica Journey

Everyone should check out Jessica Journey's blog on nonprofit leadership. She is a young, professional woman, thriving in the Indianapolis nonprofit sector. As a full-time grad student, she started a blog to make herself more attractive to nonprofit employers. Here's what Jessica had to say about the benefits of starting a nonprofit blog.

How has your blog helped you build your personal brand?

I view my blog as one tool (of many) for building my personal brand. Each tool has its place in the building process. The blog demonstrates that I am knowledgeable about my field and can think critically about interesting issues. The blog itself indicates that I value the effective use of technology. The blog's dynamic nature allows me to constantly shape and mold my personal brand.

The very process of developing the blog (and website) has forced me to answer some critical questions about my personal brand. For example, what are my areas of expertise? That is, am I writing enough about particular topics: diversity or organ donation or fundraising? And, what is the quality of my writing and ideas - in comparison to others writing about similar topics? Another important question: what is my style or tone of voice? Am I always going to provide "the right answer" to the problem? How much of my personal life am I going to reference? How do I effectively express my perspective?

How have you used your blog to enhance your nonprofit career?

- *It has helped reinforce prior contacts. For example, a former colleague was flattered when I asked her to review the blog and webpage design. She offered some helpful feedback. Then, it was quite easy to reconnect over coffee.*

- *I've been able to highlight work that I am doing with others. People enjoy being blogged about!*

- *The blog has made me more accountable to staying informed about the latest hot topic in the news or the most recent research article. It is motivation for advancing my professional knowledge.*

- *The blog has increased the number of questions I get from friends and acquaintances about the nonprofit sector. I have received more (than normal) requests for small consulting jobs. (I credit this to always posting on Facebook about my latest blog post.)*

- *Developing the blog has also increased my knowledge about website design and Internet traffic. These are yet more skills to offer to a nonprofit employer!*

Tip 19: Look Like a Leader

Thus far, this chapter may make branding feel like something that you only do online. *Au contraire, mon frère* — your personal brand is most visible in person. You can do a ton of work on your online brand, but if you don't match that brand in person, it's all for nothing. How you look and how you sound are important elements of your brand.

The popular British show-turned-book-turned-TLC show *What Not to Wear* actually gives good advice about how to dress professionally. Sadly, it must be noted that many of the participants on the American show are folks turned in by their co-workers for dressing inappropriately or sloppily. Obviously, some people need help picking out their outfits — just like in kindergarten! But really, proper dress goes a long way in the workforce.

The website www.corporette.com is an excellent resource on fashion for young professionals. A top tip from the fashion experts: dress to fit in with the atmosphere of your workplace. If business casual is the norm at work, wearing a suit every day will make you stick out like a sore thumb. For the first few days on the job, though, don't dress too casually, even if the boss wears flip-flops. When preparing for an interview and deciding what to wear, do some research on the organization. If casual dress is the norm, nice slacks and a blouse or dress shirt may be more appropriate than a suit.

Whatever your organizational culture, always be dressed for a meeting or have a backup outfit in your office, cubicle, or car. It also makes sense to keep an emergency kit in the office (toothpaste, makeup, deodorant, mints, perfume, etc.) so you can be ready for that unexpected invite to a lunch or evening event.

If you are terminally fashion-impaired, shops like Nordstrom and Macy's offer professional shopper services for free. Engaging a professional shopper will actually save you money because the professional is, well, professional. He or she will help you choose a mix and match wardrobe that is versatile, fits your budget, and helps project the image you hope to portray. Personal shoppers also have access to pre-season sales to help you get a jump on the latest styles.

Last but not least, how you speak and what you speak about are important parts of looking like a leader.

Once, Rosetta was in a meeting with about 20 other nonprofit leaders. Before the meeting got started, attendees went around the table and introduced themselves and their organizations. They went all around the room until they got to the intern who had been assigned to coordinate the meeting. When it was his turn to speak and introduce himself, he raised his head meekly and said, "Oh, I'm just here to take notes for the meeting." No matter what perception the attendees had already made about him, at that moment he deemed himself completely insignificant. He made it seem as if even his *name* was of no importance to anyone, since he did not even share what it was. He really missed an opportunity to shine while the spotlight was right on him. For the record, someone laughed at his response, then asked him if he had a name. Apparently it was Matthew.

So it's important to speak clearly and confidently in small and large group settings. Get your introduction down pat, as it is often people's first impression of you. Also think about how you refer to your current position. Do you say, "I just write grants for Girl Scouts, it's no big deal," or do you say, "I lead Girl Scouts' corporate and foundation fundraising efforts." When you speak with confidence and define your own areas of leadership, people take notice!

Chapter 5: Practice Authentic Leadership

"Becoming a leader is synonymous with becoming yourself. It is precisely that simple, and it is also that difficult." — *Warren Bennis*

As you advance in your career, it's important that you exhibit leadership in the various roles that you decide to play. Many nonprofit professionals assume that just because they have the experience and the skills required to do the job, they should automatically reap the benefits of a higher salary, better benefits, flexible work arrangements, and the like. But the reality is that you have to prove your value to your organization first. You have to demonstrate your skills and use them to lead within and beyond your job description.

What follows are several tips for practicing leadership, in a way that is effective and authentic for you.

Tip 20: Do Your Job and Do it Well

None of these other tips will help you move forward in your career if you aren't doing your current job well. You know what it takes to do well in your current position, so make sure you do it. Here are some things you should be doing, regardless of your title:

Know your job description

This is the absolute bare minimum that you have committed to doing in your position. If your position has changed, make sure that your job description has changed as well; otherwise you may be evaluated on things that are no longer your responsibility or, on the flipside, *not* evaluated on important pieces of your workload.

Know your boss's priorities and make them yours

If you are not lightening your boss's workload, you are not doing your job. Figure out what things keep your boss up at night and spend a good chunk of your time working on those issues. It is also important that you know what your executive director and board care about as well. Keeping your eye on the bigger picture and making a difference in your area of responsibility are keys to you being successful in the long run.

Stay on top of your work

Finding ways to be more efficient in your current job responsibilities gives you time to work on the bigger picture tasks. To make more time, start getting rid of time wasters (do you really need to check sports scores or gossip websites six times a day?) and make a list of the three most important things that you have to do each day to keep you focused on what's really important, rather than what's just urgent. For more hints on how to be more efficient at work, check out the book *Four Hour Work Week* by Tim Ferriss.

Play office politics

To be really effective at work, you need to know where real power exists in your organization and make sure you stay on the good side on those power brokers (aka HR lady, office party coordinator, or the CEO's administrative assistant).

Under promise and over deliver

When you make bold claims about your ability to complete a task and then aren't able to follow through, it makes you look incompetent. If you think something will take you two days to complete, say it will take three days. It gives you the time to deal with unexpected setbacks and when you get the project done early you look like, well, a nonprofit rockstar!

Alternative advice

Be part of the forgiveness sisters, not the permission sisters. Often you can't accomplish what you really need to do in your organization because of bureaucratic hoops or an overly cautious boss who always plays out the worst-case scenario for any idea that you might have. So sometimes it's necessary to move something forward without asking for permission first, Usually people are happy with the end result, even if they may not have approved the idea in the first place.

Break these bad habits and watch your career soar

These are the things that won't get you fired but will drive everyone around you crazy, so fix them before they become a real problem:

Playing with technology

Are you always playing with your Blackberry during meetings or, even worse, forget to turn off your cell phone when you leave your desk? Nothing irritates co-workers and your boss more than your "It's Raining Men" ring tone going off repeatedly while you are on another floor.

Always being late

You can be the most talented person in your organization but if you are habitually late, it reflects badly on you as a professional. Make sure that you always get to meetings a minute or two early (with something to do as you wait for all of the other people in your office who are habitually late). Being on time shows that you care about the time of your co-workers, and it also means that you don't miss out on important details.

Having a disgusting work area

Having empty chip bags, moldy coffee cups, and paper higher than eye level is not endearing. (Putting up news clippings in your office that say that disorganized people are more creative also doesn't help.) Keep your work area clean and only take out work that you can complete over the course of the day. Messy work areas don't make it look like you are busy — it looks like you are in over your head.

Always coming to your boss with problems and no solutions

Lots of people ask questions to get out of responsibility if something goes wrong. Then you always have the easy out: "You told me to do it this way." If you are facing a challenge and need your boss's advice, first brainstorm a list of possible solutions and bring your more preferred solution to your boss. You still get approval, but you have put some thought into it before you take up someone else's time.

Tip 21: Join a Nonprofit Board of Directors

Every nonprofit professional should serve on a board of directors at some point. If you plan to stay in the nonprofit field, you should see the work from all angles, especially the governance side. But more importantly, if you aspire to be a CEO or other leadership position, board experience will prove to be invaluable to you.

Here's why:

- Board membership can bring credibility to your reputation and help you gain respect from older colleagues.

- Serving on a board will allow you to hone skills you may not be able to learn at work in your current nonprofit role.

- While there may be a gray ceiling in your organization, on boards, there are plenty of leadership positions available — you can lead one of the committees or serve as an officer.

- Being a board member forces you to become knowledgeable about many different areas of nonprofit management, including finance, human resources, fundraising, legal issues, and ethics.

- You can build a strong network through your connections with other board members. You will likely meet fellow board members who you may not have otherwise crossed paths with.

- Serving on a board will help you gain the leadership skills you didn't learn in college or grad school — how to make that judgment call, when to speak up even when it's unpopular, and how to build consensus.

But before you take the plunge, make sure you do your due diligence. You don't want to go wasting your good talent on a cause or organization that's not a good fit for you.

Understand the roles and responsibilities of a board member

The best place to learn about all the different responsibilities of being a nonprofit board member is on the BoardSource website. You want to make sure you can sign on to each one of them. The experience can be rewarding, but being on a board takes hard work and integrity just like a full-time job.

Don't be afraid you won't be able to raise money

Now you may not be Mama Moneybucks, but if you can't make a significant donation as a board member, it's really not that difficult to raise money from others to fulfill your commitment to the organization. One year, Rosetta asked her friends to donate $26 to one of the nonprofits she served with in honor of her 26th birthday. She raised over $600, an amount that she wouldn't have been able to give personally, but was able to raise from her network.

Learn about the experiences of other board members

There is a really fun, interactive online tutorial called Nonprofit Board Basics from CompassPoint. The training is informative, free, and applicable to anyone thinking about joining a nonprofit board. Boardsource has also recently launched a blog called Board Life Matters as a national sounding board designed to inspire and engage the next generation in nonprofit board service. The site offers a great opportunity to read the real-life stories of young nonprofit board members.

Find board openings on boardnetUSA

A simple first step for you to take would be to create an account and profile at boardnetUSA to find listed board opportunities in your area. It only takes about 20 minutes to fill in the requested information, especially if you take a little time beforehand to think about the kind of nonprofit you want to work with and the skills you want to utilize.

Don't hesitate to contact the organization directly

If there's a cause or nonprofit you're interested in already, don't be afraid to call them directly and express your interest in board membership. Nonprofits are always looking for good board members. The best person to reach out to would be the CEO or executive director, who will be able to inform you of any openings and the process for throwing your name in the ring. You'll never know until you ask, so put yourself out there!

Rosetta joined her first nonprofit board in 2007, and it was the best leadership training she ever had. Of course, many nonprofit leaders already realize the benefits that board membership can provide for their career. For them, the next question they always ask is: How do I get on a board? Why would any nonprofit want such a young person as a board member? I don't have any wealthy friends or connections! How would I raise money for the organization?

It's then that you should think back on leadership guru Margaret Wheatley's definition of a leader:

"Leader: anyone who wants to help, who is willing to step forward to make a difference in the world."

That's you! If you have the desire and passion to serve as a board member, there are thousands of organizations that would be happy to have you.

Sometimes you can find nonprofit board openings right within your professional network. Carole Carlson has served on the Board of Interfaith Works (an organization that provides services to the homeless and low-income population) in Maryland for several years. She started out by volunteering on one of the Board committees, and after serving for a year or so, was asked to join the Board. The opening on the committee was advertised in her professional association's monthly magazine, but contacting the executive director would have been just as effective. This particular organization frequently draws board members from the ranks of its committees. Furthermore, serving on the committee gave her an opportunity to be sure that she would be proud to be associated with the organization as a board member, before making that commitment.

Tip 22: Lead a Committee

There is a difficult catch-22 when you want to become a manager. Almost every management position requires that you must have management experience to apply and yet you don't have management experience because you aren't a manager. There is, however, one possible answer to this almost unanswerable riddle: committee leadership. Running a committee gets you most of the important parts of being a manager. It is the best type of stretch assignment (Tip #26), because you get to lead a team of people and you are responsible for a specific deliverable.

Within your own organization, there may be many opportunities to lead initiatives. Committees are a great place to start because you can often manage people, budgets, and project outcomes. You also get a chance to interact with staff that you may not normally get to work with. This is especially important if you would like to move up in your current organization. You have a lot more credibility with your executive director if people from many parts of your organization say that you are doing a great job. Another benefit of leading a committee is that lots of people don't step up for committee leadership (otherwise known as "not-my-job-itis"). This is where you can really shine. Here are some skills that you will strengthen by leading a committee:

People management

This is the biggest benefit of committee leadership if you don't have experience managing staff. You are responsible for making sure that your team works well together, that they are well informed, and that everyone has assignments that tie to their unique skills. Sounds like a "manager" to us.

Managing deadlines

You learn important project management skills when you lead a committee. You are in charge of developing appropriate deadlines to make sure that everyone has the information or final products that they need to do their part of the committee's work. You also need to have the big picture in mind, as well as knowing all of the individual pieces that make up that bigger picture.

Ultimate responsibility for success or failure

If you are leading a committee, the buck stops with you. Learning the special skill of accepting the blame when something goes wrong, as well as giving the credit when something goes right, can be practiced here. Don't forget to list committee leadership and related accomplishments in your year-end summary that you provide to your boss before your review. Committee leadership may not be a core part of your job, but it is an important part of your contribution to your organization.

Here are some types of committees that you may find in your organization:

- Strategic planning committee
- Emergency preparedness
- Staff recognition
- Staff service day

- Holidays or celebrations
- Special committee to deal with new law or policy change (i.e. new 990 requirements)
- Computer systems change
- Securing a new vendor
- Annual report committee
- Special fundraising event
- Staff training
- New staff orientation
- Bring Your Child to Work day
- Diversity committee
- Evaluation
- Committee tied to a special grant

There are also more informal committees that you can lead at work. When Trista was a program officer at a community foundation, she started a lunchtime book club that identified and read management books applicable to the nonprofit sector. This allowed her to work across departments and stay up-to-date on trends in the field.

Leading a committee has many benefits. It also allows you to have a different viewpoint of your organizations' priorities and constraints, colleagues can see you in a different light, and you can stretch leadership muscles in a low-risk environment. The next time the opportunity to lead a committee comes up, don't be afraid to raise your hand.

How to lead a meeting

There is no more painful calculation than looking around a conference room during a boring, nonproductive meeting and figuring out how much it is costing in staff time for everyone to be there. Personal estimates have run from $190 for a small meeting that only lasted one painful hour to an all-day retreat where nothing was accomplished and it cost $5,100 in staff time.

If you are leading a committee, here are some strategies to make your meeting time more productive:

Have a clear agenda

Standing meetings with no purpose are the reason why so many people think meetings are a waste of time. Set a clear agenda before the meeting and give people time to add their own agenda items. The agenda should also include the goal of the meeting, so everyone is clear on what needs to be accomplished.

Make the time clear

Have clear start and ending times and stick to them. Don't wait 20 minutes for everyone to show up. If you get started on time, people that are often late will start to come on time because they know that you respect their time, so they'll respect yours.

Determine who has to be there

Some meetings may only need to have some of the team members there. It is better to proactively think about who needs to be at each meeting and only invite people that are key to that specific discussion.

Decide if the meeting really needs to happen

If the core purpose of a meeting is to "check in" about a project, save everybody the wasted time and have a document that summarizes where everyone is rather than making them sit through a painful meeting where only a minute or two is relevant to their part of the project.

Good meetings are the result of good leadership. Take the initiative and make it the meeting timely, useful, and relevant for all participants. They'll appreciate their time being used wisely and you'll get what you need from your committee.

Tip 23: Cultivate a Slash Career

Marci Alboher's fabulous book, *One Person/Multiple Careers: A New Model for Work/Life Success,* is filled with stories of "slashes," people who have created multiple careers in their lives, such as a lawyer/filmmaker, a hip-hop artist/investment banker, a minister/lawyer, a rabbi/comic, even a nonprofit director/accountant. Marci shares practical tips for people who want to add another career to their repertoire to fulfill a passion, make more money, or both. It's really an empowering look at how you can "custom blend" your careers instead of being stuck with one label or getting pigeonholed into one role. The successful stories of the slashes in the book show that you can have more than one interest and try on different hats, and in the process become more fulfilled and financially stable. Some look at their "slash" as a part-time job, some build an entire second career.

Marci's book provides insight for those who work in the nonprofit sector who gripe (with reason) that they don't make nearly enough money. Newsflash: The rate of pay is not going to change anytime soon, so assuming you can't change the system, adding a slash career could help pay the bills. Moreover, many nonprofit professionals burn out after just a few years because they view their day job as their only option of providing a stable financial future for themselves. Marci's book assures us that this is not necessarily the case. You can "slash" your life and become more self-sufficient and fulfilled as a nonprofit employee. Let us tell you about a few nonprofit slashes we know:

- Kevin, a development director/yoga instructor

- Ben, a communications director/aerobics teacher

- Rebecca, a program manager/property manager

- Eric, a program manager/artist/graphic designer

- Carol, a program director/financial planning consultant

All of these people are living out their values and earning a better living while working in the nonprofit sector. They also seem more satisfied with their lives because they get to be well-rounded. They get to work in all of the areas they love and increase their income at the same time. Their day jobs provide the stability, health insurance, and connection to an organization, while their other endeavors allow them to be more creative and bring every aspect of themselves into their work. If you've been stuck in a nonprofit career rut or are thinking about switching jobs just to earn $5,000 more a year, we'd encourage you to think about cultivating a slash career, especially if you want to do the following:

Earn supplemental income

Working part-time at anything can add more moola to your bank account. Just because you're a nonprofit employee doesn't mean you can't have another job on the side to make ends meet or pay for that dream vacation. Why don't you stop working so many late nights and weekends and devote some of that time to another paid position? Or, consider starting your own small business based on your other talents or interests.

Explore your other passions

Adding a slash to your life can open up exciting doors beyond your nonprofit role. How many people do you know that talk about things that they used to love in college like playing music, doing art, or writing poetry? If you've always had an interest, this might just be the time to pursue it as an additional career. Rosetta's mom got an MBA and landed a plum job in the corporate consulting world, but realized her heart wasn't in it. After developing a personal mission statement, she discovered that what she really wanted to do was get back into being a fitness trainer. She studied the certification materials for three months, passed the required tests, and set herself up to train clients as a slash career. She is just one example. The sky is the limit for you. For every interest, there is a slash career just waiting to be found.

Develop leadership skills to use in your nonprofit job

Being the boss in your slash career can help you build the confidence to practice leadership in your nonprofit role.

People who have their own business can be more decisive in their day jobs because they've obtained leadership experience in another setting. No matter what slash you choose, you are in charge of it, and that attitude can carry over into your regular working life and allow you to think more like a leader.

If you're thinking about cultivating a slash career, you may want to check out other resources from Marci at www.heymarci.com.

Tip 24: Polish Your Public Speaking Skills

Commonly quoted surveys say that more people are afraid of public speaking than are afraid of death. It's time to get over this irrational fear because being confident when you speak in public (or even when you speak up in meetings in the office) will increase your credibility and boost your visibility, two key factors to moving up. Instead of hiding from speaking opportunities, seek them out! Many professional associations, civic clubs (Rotary, Women's Leagues, etc.), or even high school and college classes are hungry for new speakers with an interesting topic to cover. If your nonprofit is part of the United Way, for instance, there is often a voluntary speaker bureau that promotes member agencies. Actively seek out these opportunities to boost your confidence and increase your experience speaking in public.

April Clark, a marketing communications coordinator for a nonprofit renewable energy educational organization, is a great example of someone who has gotten over this fear and thrived. Once terrified of public speaking (giving a terrible speech that makes you lose the student body presidency to your ex-boyfriend can do that), April has taken getting over stage fright to the extreme. She grabs the microphone whenever she gets a chance and is now a stand-up comedian in addition to her day job. She has performed her act at conferences and other industry events. April says:

"I work in the solar industry and once people discover I'm a comic, they want me to lighten up the crowd with my humor. My secret is to consistently get on stage whenever I have the chance, whether I'm emceeing a festival, doing stand-up at a club or party, or speaking up at a women's networking luncheon. If there's a microphone (and sometimes not a microphone, just a spotlight) I see an opportunity to improve my stage presence and public speaking skills."

Here are some tips to boost your confidence when you are speaking in public.

Practice, practice, practice

Practicing your presentation while staring at yourself in the mirror is only going to stress you out. You will notice many tiny little things that will drive you nuts and that the audience won't notice at all. Develop the loose notes for your presentation and talk to yourself and to friends and family about the topic that you will be covering. That will help you determine which parts of the presentation you are really comfortable with and which parts need some more work. It will also help you determine what sort of questions your audience will have after your presentation.

Shawn Dove, an experienced public speaker and campaign manager for the Black Men and Boys program at the Open Society Institute, said that he has a set of stories and examples that he always uses in presentations. He does that because he is very comfortable with the material and because it has been tried in the past he knows that it will be well received by the audience. Find your own tried-and-true examples that you are always prepared to use.

When you are giving a public presentation, make sure that you have at least 3-5 sound bites that are interesting and "tweetable" in 140 characters or less. Your presentation can quickly reach beyond the ballroom if you give the audience short, catchy ideas that they can share on social media sites.

Know your audience

When you first agree to speak at a session, ask the organizers who they think will be in your audience, the expected audience size, and what experience the audience has with your topic. This will help you craft your presentation in a way that will meet more of their needs.

A common mistake of conference presenters is that they write the description for their session months before the actual conference and don't refer back when they are writing up their presentation. If an audience has been promised something specific in a session description, they will be disappointed if you don't cover that in your remarks. The mass exodus that usually happens about 10 minutes into a conference session usually has to do with an audience member thinking that they were going to hear about a specific topic in the session and it seems like that isn't going to happen, so they vote with their feet.

Experienced public speakers often ask a question or two in the beginning of their session to gauge their audience so they can reframe their remarks for the audience's needs. Some examples of framing phrases:

- "How many of you have been in the nonprofit sector for 5 years or less?"

- "How many of you have a social media plan already?"

- "Raise your hand if you came here because you have questions about the 990."

This type of audience participation will let you know if your remarks are on track for the demographics of the audience, for their skill level, or for their interest in the topic you are discussing. You are also getting them engaged in your presentation right away.

Melissa James, the public relations and marketing director for Downtown Hampton Child Development Center in Virginia, says, "I look at public speaking more like a conversation with new friends — as though they had just asked me to tell them about the place where I work, and I was answering. And as I've learned more and more about my organization, it has become easier to tailor what I say to the flow of the presentation and the audience's responses. I've learned to 'read' the audience and alter my direction to their comfort as I go."

Give them a roadmap

Cliff Atkinson, author of *Beyond Bullet Points*, is a presentation expert. He teaches readers to tell a story with their presentations through a recognizable story structure that you are familiar with if you have ever watched a movie. His presentation structure has three acts: set up the story from the audience's perspective, develop the action, and set up the resolution. This is a traditional story arc where there is some sort of problem or conflict that the audience cares about and a resolution that the audience is on the edge of their seats waiting for.

Right now you may be thinking, "I give presentations about the retention statistics of my mentoring program. No one is sitting on the edge of their seats waiting to hear those numbers." You're right; no one is waiting to hear you say:

> 75% of children are matched within 6 months, the average match length is 4 years, and matched youth report an 86% satisfaction rate with their mentorship experience.

Ugh, that makes us bored just typing that. Next time, you might say something like:

> Angie is the youngest of 5 children and her mom works two jobs to make sure that her children are able to live in a safe neighborhood. Because of the sacrifices that her mom is making to give her and her brother and sisters a better life, Angie doesn't get a lot of one-on-one attention. After hearing about the Big Brothers and Big Sisters program, she immediately asked her mom to sign her up. She waited patiently for 6 months for a big sister and when Trina became her Big, a whole new world opened up for her. She learned to rollerblade, saw Lake Superior for the first time, and even found out that she is a natural poet. They have now been matched for 4 years and Angie was recently accepted to Howard University and will be the first in her family

to attend college. Trina couldn't be prouder of her and neither could I.

Help your audience get engaged in what you are saying, so that they are along for the ride with the characters in your story. They are more likely to enjoy your presentation and remember more of what you said.

Show that you care

Chances are you're probably pretty passionate about the work that you do. Make sure that passion is visible to your audience. Danielle Nierenberg, an expert on livestock and sustainability for the Worldwatch Institute, says, "I used to be terrified of public speaking, but now I just remind myself that I am talking about topics that I am passionate about. I think that my passion and enthusiasm come through naturally."

An overly structured speech does nothing but pull you away from that passion, so you might as well be reading the newspaper out loud. Develop a loose outline for yourself that has your key points but doesn't lay out every sentence. This helps you speak more naturally about the topic and allows your passion to shine through.

Don't let your looks be a distraction

A hole in your nylons or a stain on your shirt or lettuce in your teeth are big distractions that prevent the audience from listening to your message. Before you go on stage or in front of a room of people, take a quick restroom break to give yourself a once-over in the mirror.

Strengthening your speaking presence on the stage and in the office will help you effectively get your point across and raise the profile of you and the issues that you care about. If you are still nervous and want to polish your speaking, find a speech coach. Many actors do this as a side job and can help you increase your ability to project your voice and to emphasize points by varying your voice. Even a few sessions can make a big difference. It's time to let go of this irrational fear and grab the mic.

Who's your speaking mentor?

A speaking mentor is a visible public speaker that you look to to help guide the development of your own speaking style. This doesn't mean that you copy their mannerisms and become a Barack Obama impersonator. It just means that you figure out what works for their personal speaking style and then interpret that into something that feels right for you. Here are some examples of speaking mentors:

Majora Carter

Environmental Activist; MacArthur Genius
Speaking Style: Inspirational, conversational
Look: Very fashionable, natural, and approachable
Technique: Storytelling, combined with hard hitting statistics and still photos of the neighborhoods that she talks about in her presentations.

Steve Jobs

President of Apple
Speaking Style: Technical but with an approachable feel
Look: Always wears blue jeans and a black turtleneck
Technique: Clear themes, smooth transitions, and the element of surprise to unveil new features

Jan Masaoka

Director and Editor-in-Chief of Blue Avocado; leading thinker on nonprofits
Speaking Style: Funny, with great ideas on how to improve nonprofits
Look: Funky but very professional
Technique: Traditional keynote with expressive hand gestures

Who is your speaking mentor? What pieces of their style would you like to use in your own presentations? What will you change to make it more you?

Tip 25: Ask for Feedback

If you don't know how you're doing, it's next to impossible to improve your performance, let alone your skills. Here are some tips to solicit feedback in your nonprofit job.

Ask for it and ask often

Who wants to wait six months to a year to know if they need to brush up on their organizational skills or interpersonal communications? Set a meeting with your boss and let him or her know you're looking for some constructive feedback to help you do your job better in between reviews. Your boss will be impressed with your initiative and you'll reap the benefit of knowing exactly what you need to do right now to get ahead.

Handle negative criticism with maturity

If your boss, a board member, or even your co-worker criticizes you for something you don't even agree with, it can be tough to swallow. Rosetta recalls her first-ever performance evaluation at a nonprofit job. Her boss told her she was "too timid" when she answered the phones as part of her receptionist duties. Rosetta's first thought was, "Timid? I'll show her timid!" But when she probed deeper to ask how she could improve, her boss simply suggested that she speak more loudly when greeting callers and visitors. What started off as offensive criticism to Rosetta turned out to be very simple feedback that she could act upon immediately.

Tip 26: Do a Stretch Assignment

Rosetta first heard about the "stretch assignment" concept while on a panel with former Annie E. Casey Foundation executive Patrick Corvington. Patrick had suggested that emerging nonprofit leaders embark on stretch assignments to advance their careers. Rosetta was intrigued to learn that a "stretch assignment" was simply an activity that requires a worker to take a leap beyond her comfort zone and, in the process, pick up new skills.

What does this really mean? In your current position there are things that are required, and then there are things that you can do to move your skills to the next level. A stretch assignment is something that makes you exercise skills you rarely use or helps you build new skills. You could stay within your comfort zone forever, but the real growth comes when you take a personal and professional risk by doing something greater than your current skills set.

The demands of stretch assignments require you to step out of your comfort zone, develop new skills, and cope with the anxiety and stress that comes from taking risks. But with each new stretch assignment (it's not just a one-time deal), you get more resourceful, resilient, and better able to handle the stress of uncertainty. That means with each assignment, you bring an even greater ability to manage the project. This makes you a more competent and confident leader.

Possible stretch assignments are around every corner. The first thing to do is to let your supervisor know that you want to contribute beyond your current job description or you could even describe the skills that you are trying to build (project management, fundraising, budgeting, etc.). Then start to look around your organization for places where more people power would be helpful. Is there a process that is inefficient? Is there a program that needs some attention? Is there a part of the organization's strategic plan that nobody has had time to work on? A two-for-one would be identifying a stretch assignment that would be a direct benefit to your supervisor (see Tip #32 on Managing Up).

Trista's most useful stretch assignment was when she volunteered to lead her department's strategic planning efforts. Then, when she interviewed for the Executive Director position at Headwaters, she was able to reference that experience. The skills that she learned with her previous employer allowed her to successfully manage Headwaters' strategic planning process, which started just a few months after she began.

If you are still having a tough time thinking of a stretch assignment, the Leadership Development Centre offers a great list of tangible examples of stretch assignments for public sector leaders:

- Leading or implementing a new or important project – a culture change, a new human resource strategy, a new community project or service

- Organizing a rally or conference

- Staffing a board committee within your organization

- Being accountable for managing people to achieve specific outcomes within a given timeline

- Taking on a significant project of work that presents new learning and challenges

- Completing a qualification or significant learning opportunity

- Working or managing a cross-cultural team

- Turning around a failing operation

- Taskforce assignment or special project that involves an increase in scope (e.g. budget, number of staff or complexity of role)

- Leading an important event or meeting

- Supervising an intern or volunteer

- Getting involved in your organization's strategic planning process

And stretch assignments don't have to just happen at work. You could also:

- Join a board at another nonprofit

- Organize a bartering co-op in your neighborhood

- Help a candidate run for elected office

- Run for elected office yourself

- Develop an algebra tutoring program for your child's school

- Fundraise for your favorite nonprofit

The purpose is to go beyond your normal skills and figure out what additional things you are good at and passionate about.

What do you get out of stretching?

- Confidence in your abilities and skills
- Clarity of personal passion and vision for social change
- Better understanding of how to manage nonprofit operations more effectively
- Change management skills
- Skills in influencing others
- Leadership development by "doing"

What happens if you don't stretch?

- No personal or professional growth
- Skills don't improve or stay stagnant
- Your boss's or peer's perception of you won't change
- Your strategic thinking abilities aren't developed
- Leadership skills aren't exercised
- Fear in trying out new or challenging experiences
- Lack of opportunities to develop your own vision for a new future
- No sense of the complexities involved in enabling change to happen

Tip 27: Speak Up!

More nonprofit leaders, especially young people, should be sharing their ideas and innovation to help move organizations forward. Now is not the time to be quiet if we have ways to improve the way we do the work of social change. But we have to recognize that we do need to build up the kind of skills and confidence to help us do what leaders do: speak up! There is too much at stake for us not to. Below are some ideas that might help you build your ability to speak up for what you believe in as you move from entry level to leadership.

Volunteer to speak at an event or conference

Rosetta's very first speaking engagement was as a panelist for the *Who's Got Next? Addressing the Leadership Crisis Among African-American Organization*s conference. She looked at the current speaker list, and realized that there were no young nonprofit leaders slated to talk about their experiences. So she emailed the conference organizer with a link to her blog and her bio. The conference organizers quickly followed up with her for a phone conversation and ultimately added Rosetta to the panel. Don't wait for someone to ask you to participate in an event or conference; the first step may be you reaching out to them! It's great exposure, and you get the chance to share your thought leadership with a captive audience. Be sure to keep your kick-butt bio handy for when you see an opportunity to volunteer your time and expertise.

Be an advocate

The economic crisis and its effect on nonprofits offers a myriad of timely opportunities to advocate for funding and policies related to the sustainability of the sector. Just because you are not a CEO doesn't mean you have to stay behind your desk. Go testify to your local government officials about legislation that would affect your organization or your clients. Volunteer to assist your advocacy director if your organization has one. Write letters to your state representatives to show your support or opposition to policies that affect your cause. You may also consider joining the Council of Nonprofits. The organization does a great job of monitoring legislation affecting nonprofits and helping to mobilize nonprofit professionals to speak up where it really matters.

If there are issues that you care about that are outside of the scope of your organization's work, don't let that stop you. Just because you work for the Humane Society doesn't mean you aren't passionate about alternative teacher certification or water issues in Kenya. Take the time to write a letter to the editor, start a social media campaign, or host a fundraiser for a candidate that will move that issue forward. Each organization has different rules about staff members lobbying outside of work hours. Figure out what your organization's rules are and then work on the change you want to see in the world.

Tip 28: Mentor Someone Else

No matter where you are in your career, there is always someone is who is on the part of the career path that you were on a few years ago that would benefit from your insights. Being a mentor gives you the ability to help someone else, and you never know if that person you are mentoring will become your board chair or your boss in the future.

Melissa Johnson, executive director of the Neighborhood Funders Group (and a nonprofit rockstar in her own right), was a mentor to her very first intern at a community foundation in North Carolina. The mentee, Cecelia Thompson, was then hired on at the foundation and soon after became executive director of the Guilford Green Foundation ... even before Melissa, her mentor, became an executive director!

Melissa says, "I have been so impressed with her leadership! I continue to help her strategize on major career moves. I have gotten so much out of this mentoring relationship. It has helped me practice what I preach."

Always be open to informational interviews

These interviews only take a little bit of time and expand your professional network greatly. Always say yes when someone asks.

Be an informal mentor

Sometimes people want to learn a skill that you have or more information about a topic that you know a lot about. Just a few meetings might be what it takes to share that with someone who is interested. Just set a clear end time when this sort of relationship starts.

Be a full deal mentor

If you do become a more official mentor, be clear with the mentee what they want to get out of the relationship, how long you are going to meet (during a school year, until they find a job, for the next six months, etc.). Keep your promises to your mentee — better to under promise and over deliver rather than disappoint your mentee by cancelling meetings and phone calls when other things come up.

If you are proactively looking for a mentee, check out your alma mater or local professional association. They may have a list of students or members that are looking for mentors. You can also volunteer to work closely with your organization's interns or VISTA volunteers.

Being a good mentor is a great first step for being a good manager. Be open to opportunities that will help you build your mentorship muscles.

Chapter 6: Plan for Balance

In our experiences, it's pretty tough to even think about taking on more leadership if you can barely handle the responsibilities that you currently have on your plate. While we encourage career advancement in the nonprofit sector, we don't want to see you rocking your career at the expense of everything else in your life. This chapter covers strategies for planning a balanced career, while Chapter 7 follows with advice on how to move on up once you're good and ready.

Tip 29: Develop a Personal Mission Statement

Every nonprofit has a mission statement to guide their work. So, why shouldn't you? It is truly an eye-opening process to write out your goals and values for your life and then compare them to how you actually balance your priorities. There's something really powerful and empowering about being able to say 'yes' or 'no' to opportunities that come into your life and work based on how you want to live out your personal values. But what, exactly, is a personal mission statement?

Productivity website Dumb Little Man offers this great definition:

"Your personal mission statement should be a concise representation of what's most important to you, what you desire to focus on, what you want to achieve, and, ultimately, who you want to become. In its purest form, it's an approach to your life, one that allows you to identify a focus of energy, creativity, and vision in living a life in support of your inner-most beliefs and values. Also remember that your mission will change over time as you and your life change."

There are many ways to go about creating your own personal mission statement, but we will highlight an easy three-step process here. You should take as much time as you need to reflect and write out your mission statement. It can be short-term or long-term, and should encompass your goals for both work and life. The process and the final statement can help you make many different kinds of decisions about how you will lead and live your life.

Step 1: Identify your values

What matters most to you in life? What matters most to you right now? Take at least 15 minutes to jot down a free-for-all list of everything that means a lot to you. Be as specific as possible. To get you started, here are just a few examples of values might include:

- Achievement, fame, advancement, leadership
- Money, power, authority, economic security
- Having a family, children, love, community, friendships
- Nature, religion, public service, ecological awareness, healthy living, physical challenge
- Democracy, civic involvement, wisdom, integrity, truth

Step 2: Identify your goals

Once you've reflected on what matters most to you, then take at least 15 minutes to think about how you want to be remembered. What do you most want to contribute to the world, and what goals do you want to accomplish for yourself and your career? What kind of difference do you want to make before you die? Your goals can also be related to how you want to go about building your career, and of course you will have more than one! To get you started, here are just a few ideas of what your goals might include:

- Career aspirations
- Volunteer interests

- Ways to make social impact
- Ways you want to grow in your career or personal life

Step 3: Write your mission statement

Now that you've identified your values and your goals, you should now take at least 30 minutes to write your personal mission statement. It can be as short or as long as you think it needs to be. And remember, it will continue to change as you change over time, so don't worry about it being perfect and final. This should be a work in progress, just like you!

Here is what Rosetta's mission statement looks like:

I value education, achievement, adventure, creativity, and independence. I especially value authenticity in myself and others. I appreciate laughter, good food, music, art, poetry and black history & culture. Before I die, I want to have made a positive impact on the world for young people, women, and people of color. As a writer, professor, consultant, and volunteer, I will lead according to my values by teaching others and helping people reach their goals. I will network to stay connected to others who are living a life of purpose. In my journey to take care of others, I will not neglect my own family, friends, finances, health, or spirituality.

Tip 30: Schedule Time to Reflect

It's important to find time to reflect on where you are and where you are going. Consistent strategic thinking time is important for your everyday work. Even setting aside a consistent time three times a week to think about big issues at work will make you more effective at what you do!

During these times, pick one question that you can wrestle with. For example, how can I fix XYZ issue with my boss? Who is the best partner for our new program? What is my strategy for getting a raise? Make sure that you do this thinking somewhere that you are comfortable and bring something to capture those ideas. A journal, notecards, or even the recording feature on your phone will all work.

Strategic thinking is especially critical as you think about your long-term plans or career goals. Set aside time once per year to evaluate those goals. Key questions to consider during this time are:

- Do I like my job?

- What current challenges am I facing?

- What am I great at?

- What would I like to be doing ten years from now?

One of the biggest challenges of strategic thinking time is getting far enough from your day-to-day challenges so you can think uninterrupted. Trista's best ideas come during conference sessions, where new ideas are bound to bubble to the surface. Other people come up with great ideas while exercising or playing a sport. Here are some suggestions of other places that you can go to think deeply.

- Park

- Library

- Arboretum

- Coffee shop

- Museum

Put strategic thinking time on your calendar and selfishly guard it. It's the easiest thing to let go of, but can be the most important part of your professional development.

Patrick Cokley is a policy advisor for the Office of Disability Employment Policy at the U.S. Department of Labor. Every year since his freshman year of college he has been taking time on his birthday to reflect on the year that has passed and to do some planning for the coming year. Patrick says, "I take this time to take stock of the past year and evaluate what was positive about the past year and make moves to eliminate the negative aspects. I have found that by doing this strategic thinking I have been able to actively increase my effectiveness at work, my pay grade, and my personal career satisfaction."

Tip 31: Don't Skip Lunch

Working for social change can be both exciting and rewarding. The flip side of having an awesome nonprofit job where you get to impact people's lives, however, is that you can work *too* much and end up crashing and burning out early on in your career. But if you establish good work/life balance habits from the beginning, you can maintain your health, wellness, and sanity required to keep working in the field that you love.

Never take work home with you

It can be difficult to draw the line at work, especially when you first start a job. You want to impress your boss and colleagues, all while seeming committed to the cause. But you must remember that what you do in the beginning will set the standard for what will be expected of you in the future. So, don't take work home with you! Manage your time wisely during work hours so that you complete what you can during the allotted time. Use your time at home to spend time with friends and family, and rest up for the next day's work. Believe us, it will still be there in the morning!

Eat lunch, preferably away from your desk

Nonprofit work can get very hectic, no matter if you're in the fundraising department or on the front lines helping clients. It's easy to ignore your growling stomach when there's too much work to do in so little time. But you have to remember that everyone works better when they are adequately nourished. Please don't skip lunch. And when you do eat lunch, try to eat away from your desk and take the full lunch hour given to you. Also try to take frequent breaks during the workday to take a walk around the block. Getting outside for a moment forces both your mind and body to relax for a bit, especially from the computer screen.

Don't take on too much, too soon

Part of having a successful nonprofit career is to know what you do well, and play to your strengths. Sometimes, though, nonprofits can be understaffed and ask you to take on another role in which you have no knowledge or skill. Be willing to help out, but be sure you manage your boss' expectations of you. If you're asked to do someone else's job, there should be an understanding of how you will also be able to fulfill your current duties. Don't be afraid to challenge deadlines and continually revisit priorities because you're not Superwoman (or Superman), and you have to face reality about what you're really able to do in a day, a week, or a month.

Many nonprofit professionals complain about having too much work to do and not being compensated for it. Understand that you do have a say in how your career will play out. It's up to you whether you'll be working late all the time or starving all day long because you skipped lunch. It's up to you to do what you need to do for yourself to prevent burnout so you can stay in the nonprofit career that you love.

Tip 32: Fall Back in Love With Your Job

If you've been working in the same nonprofit job for years, it can be difficult to keep the fire alive. After a particularly bad or hectic day, it can seem impossible to stay resilient with all the challenges brought on by the economic downturn. You may already be doing the work of two positions, causing your workload to increase. All the while, you may be asking yourself, "Why am I doing this again?" Even though you may not be feeling the love right now, here are a few ways to get it back.

Volunteer

Get close to the day-to-day mission of your organization by volunteering for your nonprofit. Presumably, it's the cause that caught your eye in the first place. Sign up to be a tutor for a day with the kids you serve or feed the homeless one evening after work. If it seems like extra work, it is. But being face-to-face with the people who benefit from your nonprofit's mission can be incredibly refreshing, and make you look forward to Monday instead of dreading it.

Visit a program

What does your organization actually do for your clients? Have you ever seen it in action? Take a few hours to go visit one of your nonprofit's programs. Sit in on a financial literacy class, watch as your counselors help the unemployed craft resumes, or attend a play your arts organization is performing. The idea is to see for yourself the impact that your efforts have on others. It will make you appreciate why you do your work every day, no matter how tough it gets.

Write a passionate letter

Sit down and craft a handwritten letter to one of your donors to personally thank them for supporting your organization. Even if this is the development department's role, you can never send too many thank-you letters. Tell the donor what kind of impact their gift made and how much you love working on behalf of the people you serve.

Make a phone call

You may already be aware of the different kinds of legislation affecting your clients or your cause. It can be a powerful feeling to be an advocate for your cause by speaking out as a concerned citizen. When a bill is passed that helps you in your work, go ahead and call your local government official or congressional representative to thank them for supporting your cause. Their contact information is published right there on the Internet, and every phone call helps them to know just how important the issue is to their constituents.

Redesign your day

Maybe you're just tired of coming into the office at 8:00 a.m. If your schedule is set for you to work too early or too late, have a talk with your boss to ask if you can change it. Rosetta used to work a typical 9-to-5, but she found that she actually worked better later in the day, so she simply told her boss that she wanted to start coming in from 10am-6pm. It gave her more time to sleep in the morning, and didn't harm the organization one bit. And she was a happier employee for it.

We know, you might be thinking, "Who has time for all this?" especially if you're too busy putting fires out all day. But trust us, if you make time for balance now, it will save you from burnout later. It's never too late to fall back in love with your work.

Tip 33: Ditch the Martyr Lifestyle

"I'm worried about you," Rosetta's grandmother said. Rosetta could hear the maternal worry vibrating over the phone lines hundreds of miles away. "You never call me anymore, and you're always working. Are they paying you overtime?"

Rosetta chuckled. "No, Grandma, nonprofits don't pay overtime. Besides, I'm on salary and I'm leading this big new project. I need to work late so I can get it all together."

Her grandmother clucked. You know, that disapproving sound that only a grandmother can make. "Well, you can't do anything if you're in the hospital, and that's what's going to happen to you if you keep working so much."

A few weeks later, Rosetta found herself doubled over in bed, too sick to go to work for a week. In an instant, her fast-paced nonprofit world had come to a halt, and she could hear her grandmother's words ringing in her ear through the fog of all the medication she was taking.

Sound familiar? That's because you may also be playing the martyr role for your nonprofit. You may be scratching your head right now. Martyr role? Yes, right here in our very own nonprofit sector of helping others and empowering the powerless, many of us behave as if we are the victims within our own organizations. How many times have you heard someone say, "If I didn't kill myself working 70 hours a week for this organization, there's no way everything would get done around here." Or, "I'm so bummed I had to come in to the office last weekend to write 10 grant proposals and missed seeing my favorite band." Or our favorite, "My nonprofit takes up so much of my time, I really don't have too much of a personal life." This is all behavior consistent with the definition of a martyr: one who suffers for the sake of principle or for a particular cause.

But how can this be? Most professionals came to the nonprofit sector because they wanted to help their communities, not put themselves in misery for a job that requires long hours and low pay. But that's exactly what many of us do. We often don't realize that the work can and will get completed if you live your life like a normal person. Your nonprofit will not fall apart if you take a vacation or ask for a raise.

We know you may not have realized that you exhibit the behavior of a martyr, but if you think that by working in nonprofit, you deserve sympathy or admiration for sacrificing your own happiness, comfort, and financial security, you just might fit the bill. As a nonprofit worker, sometimes you need to get over yourself and stop playing the victim of small budgets, short staff, and weak leadership. It's not your fault, and you don't have to overcompensate for the sins of the nonprofit sector.

You might be a martyr in your nonprofit if:

- You stay later than everyone else as a commitment to "the work" or "the mission"

- You sneer at any staff who leave the office by 5 p.m.

- You think you are indispensable

- You can't remember the last time you took a real vacation (i.e. at least a week away from the office doing something utterly relaxing and totally unrelated to work)

- You come in to work even when you're sick as a dog

- You never ask for salary increases because you want to preserve as much money in the budget for the programs as possible

- You look 10 years older than you really are

Rosetta stopped to reflect on her martyr lifestyle only when someone in her family noticed. She had neglected to take care of her body, and was overworking herself for the sake of "the cause," not unlike many professionals who are stuck in this pattern. We love our jobs and our organizations so much that we let our passion consume us, and forget about taking care of ourselves. Rosetta changed many of her habits after getting hit with illness, but it really is a daily effort to set boundaries on your time and energy. Please, for goodness' sake, don't be a martyr. It's quite all right to have a life. There's no reason you need to suffer for the sake of your nonprofit's cause.

Nonprofit Rockstar: Paul Schmitz

Too many nonprofit professionals don't even use all of their vacation days. But taking time off is more important than ever in order to help you recharge your batteries and be a better leader when you return to your organization.

Paul Schmitz, CEO of Public Allies, talks about the importance of taking a vacation, even amidst the hectic pace of nonprofit work. Paul believes that taking time off helps him to be a stronger nonprofit CEO:

"I believe that the balance I try to strike makes me more effective. I have had some of my best insights and strategies emerge when I have been away from the office and unplugged from the day-to-day. And a good vacation brings me back energized and feeling excited to be back."

Tip 34: Clear Off Your Plate

In preparing for a greater level of responsibility at work, one of the things you have to do is make sure that you have the time and space for those added duties. The first step is evaluating how you are spending your time. Does it match your values? Are those activities the best use of the 168 hours that you have in a week? An eye-opening activity is writing down how you are spending time every 15 minutes for one week.

You'll be surprised at the results. Once you have done your own time study, you will have a better idea of your own personal time-wasters.

One magical tip for reducing time wasters at work is to batch tasks. Instead of doing tasks here and there throughout the day, batching is grouping those tasks and doing them all at once. For example, instead of checking your email every time your notification buzzer goes off (please go shut that off right now, it encourages you to be inefficient), you batch the emails and respond to them just once or twice per day. This will save you a ton of time and increase your ability to focus. A study of Microsoft workers found that it takes 15 minutes for employees to return to serious mental tasking after they responded to an email or an instant message. After those initial interruptions, employees often responded to other email messages or started surfing the Internet before returning to the task at hand. If you are checking email or dealing with other interruptions at work, you are limiting your ability to complete the most important tasks. Other things you can batch are: phone calls, social media time (set aside time for that Twitter deep dive that you know you are going to take), and meetings. If you do a lot of informational meetings or something similar, schedule those back to back at the same location so that you can cut back on travel time.

Work is definitely not the only place where you need to clear off your plate. Clearing the plate at home gives you the mental energy to take on new responsibilities at work. With two school-aged kids at home, Trista has had to become an expert at simplifying her home life; otherwise a leadership position in philanthropy would have been impossible. Here are some suggestions for clearing your plate at home:

Un-volunteer

When you volunteer, spend that precious time with organizations that you love, doing work that few are able to do. For example, many people can stock a food pantry, but few can write a strategic plan for one. It's all right to step away from volunteer opportunities where you don't add real value or when they are for organizations where you aren't very passionate about the cause.

Get rid of hobbies that are just habits

If your hobby doesn't reinvigorate you, then quit doing it. Just because you have always been a kite boarder or geocatcher doesn't mean you still love it. You'll save time and money. By the way, too much television or videogames can also be a habit. Reevaluate how much of your life is being dominated by "screen time."

Use those extra bits of time

Due to some breakdown in school district planning, Trista has 35 minutes between when she needs to drop her daughter off at middle school and when her son starts elementary school. It is too short of a time to go back home and too long to sit in the school parking lot. She uses this little chunk of time for grocery shopping, dropping off library books, and helping her son practice reading. If the weather is nice (a rarity in freezing cold Minnesota), they might also have time for some fun on the playground. There are probably lots of time during your week where you are waiting for karate practice to end or waiting for your train to arrive. Think ahead so you have a plan to use that time.

Batch at home

This is the same as the "batching" tip from the work section. Do all of your errands in one trip, saving gas and eliminating the back and forth. Cook big batches of food at once; it will take less time and you'll have leftovers for lunch or a meal for another day if your freezer is large enough. You can even batch entertaining! If you are having friends over for a fondue party and hosting a kid's birthday party, host them on the same weekend. You'll only have to deep-clean your house once and you can make appetizers that will work for both parties.

Kids can be the best helpers

If you're a parent, you know that keeping a well-functioning household isn't easy when you have kids running around. Teach kids to pick up after themselves and limit where they are able to have their things. Trista has a "no-toys in the living room" rule; that means that she won't step on Star Wars guys when she's trying to relax and it makes it much easier to keep that visible place in the house clean.

Bedtime routines are not just for kids

If you are unprepared, morning can be a crazy time. Get your clothes laid out for the next day, do your ironing, and pack your lunch at night. It will make your mornings much more peaceful.

Consider bringing in the professionals

Just because you *can* do something doesn't mean that you *should*. Sometimes, paying someone to clean your house, do your taxes, or mow your lawn makes more financial sense than you doing it yourself. If you could pay someone $20 an hour to mow your lawn and you get paid $75 an hour as a freelance grantwriter, hire someone and use that time to do something more productive.

Once you've cleaned off your plate you'll be surprised at how much more responsibility you'll be ready to take on in your nonprofit career.

Tip 35: Mind Your Money

Money is often an area that gets ignored by nonprofit professionals. Because we are so passionate about our work, we say things like, "I don't do this job for the money." That is all fine and dandy until you begin ignoring your financial life for too long. In the long run, the stress of not being able to manage your bills makes it more likely you will make life and career decisions based on dollars rather than on what you are truly passionate about.

Here are some ways to get your money right:

Get your credit report

Make sure that you get your free credit report at least once per year from all three of the credit report agencies. This will help you figure out if you have any errors on your report or if someone has been using your credit. You can obtain your free credit report from https://www.annualcreditreport.com/cra/index.jsp.

Know how much it costs to pay your monthly bills

Knowing is half the battle. Pull out every single paper bill that you have and check your bank statement for other automatic deductions. Make sure that you also have an idea of how much your yearly expenses cost as well. For example, if you spend $600 every year for holiday gifts, then every month you should be putting aside $50 to be able to pay for this expense. This also goes for car repairs, yearly travel, and unexpected medical or home repair bills.

Make it automatic

Bill paying can be a stressful activity, so limit the stress by putting as many of your bills as possible on auto-payment. Many banks will do this at no cost. This will ensure that your bills get paid on time, without you thinking about it constantly. Another suggestion is to set these auto-payments for the day after your paycheck arrives, then what is left in your account can be spent on flexible expenses like groceries, gas, and massages (ahhhhh).

Plan for retirement when you are entry-level

No matter how old you are, retirement should be a part of your financial plan. If your organization matches up to 4% of your salary in a 403(b) retirement account, you should be putting in that 4% as an absolute minimum. If you don't, it's like throwing away your own money. A good rule of thumb is that 10% of your salary should be put away for retirement each year. You might also think about putting half of any raises in your retirement account as well. You won't miss it and it will make a big difference in the long-term.

So, after you have gotten a handle on your financial situation, there is still a chance that you might be spending more than you make or your debt payments may be overwhelming (student loans, anyone?). Instead of burying your head in the sand or running off to work at an investment bank, think about skills that you have that might help you make some extra money on the side. Remember, "slash careers" could include contract grantwriting, tutoring, selling your handmade crafts on Etsy, or running a family-centered travel company. Slash careers are only limited by your imagination and, of course, your need to watch Lost reruns.

If you are knowledgeable about your own financial situation and you are thoughtful about the big picture, you can be more flexible in your career choices and a lot less stressed.

Ten-year financial plans

Trista and her husband developed a ten-year financial plan for their family. She says:

"Yes, I know that is so nerdy of me and is making many of you cringe at my over-planning, but whatever. Ten years gives me a clearer picture of the big things that we are working towards and makes small steps to reach those goals much more manageable. It also helps my husband and me stay on the same page when it comes to giving up small purchases now for big payoffs in the future."

Their plan includes their top five financial goals for the next 10 years, along with charts that help them track our progress on those goals. Here are some of the features of the plan:

- It includes accounts and hints on usernames and passwords so it can be easily updated.

- The plan only needs to be pulled out once a year to update and to change any current financial practices to meet the goals (e.g. increase amount they put into 401(k)).

- It doesn't just include dollar goals — it also includes things that get them excited, like becoming a benefactor to causes that they are passionate about.

Trista shares: "I spent a lot of time in the past ignoring my financial state because I thought that the more I knew, the more stressed I would be. I have finally come to a place where I understand that ignorance is not bliss and that how I spend the money that comes into my life is an important part of who I am and how I want to change the world."

Tip 36: When Work and Home Collide

Let's be real from the beginning: There is no such thing as daily work/life balance. That is just an urban legend designed to make us feel torn at work and inadequate at home. But, over a lifetime you should have a real feeling of balance and reaching your goals in both of these areas. So, since there isn't some magical way to be balanced every day, here are some strategies to make life more manageable in the long term:

Set limits

You have to determine what makes the most sense for you both at home and at work. If you have to pick kids up from daycare at 5 p.m., don't set meetings after 3 p.m. so that you are sure to get to daycare on time. If you're in a band that practices in the evenings, make sure that you set the expectation with your co-workers that you always leave the office by 5:30. People will only ask as much of you as you are willing to give. So figure out what your own line is and don't cross it.

Have a life that you look forward to

It's easy to spend your days, nights, and weekends in the office if you don't have something that you care about at home. Schedule time to develop hobbies and interests outside of work. If having a spouse or partner is important to you and you haven't yet found that special person, make sure that you leave time for those relationships to develop.

Vickie Williams, executive director of the Jeremiah Program, has always been successful at work. A few years ago when she met her husband, she made sure that she took time to get to know him better and to strengthen their relationship. She became very good at setting limits at work and no longer joined volunteer committees or added other responsibilities that would take her from home. Vickie says, "I always put my career and my organization first. Now I'm putting just as much energy into being happy at home."

Plan ahead

If you know that your family is taking a two-week vacation in the summer, make sure that you mark that time as far ahead in your calendar as possible. The same goes for school conferences, your fantasy football draft day, or the week when you harvest all of the tomatoes in your garden. If you know that you have a busy time coming up at work, get some backup for your home stuff. Do your kids need to have some extra time with their grandparents that week? Do you need to have the neighbor play with your dog? Or do you need to tell your kickball team that you can't come to practices the week your annual report is being finalized? If you think of how your home and work intersect, there will be fewer surprises and stressors.

Be efficient at work

If you spend your days gossiping about American Idol and sending email chain letters, it's not surprising that it's taking you 60 hours a week to get your work done. Start focusing on your most important tasks at the start of each day and get it done. Learning to delegate and eliminating the tasks that aren't helping you reach your career goals will also make it easier to be more efficient.

Ignore the imaginary barriers at home

Sometimes we imagine that some things are impossible because of commitments at home. Mariah Carroll Owens dreamed of going to Uganda to complete an intensive journalism practicum about HIV/AIDS in sub-Saharan Africa. She also had an elementary school-aged daughter, who would be in school during this month-long program. The expected thing to do would be to put her dream on hold until her daughter grew up or at least until summer break. Instead, Mariah talked to her daughter's principal and arranged to take her out of school for the month with a pile of homework to complete on the journey. Mariah says, "It was a life-changing experience for both of us. I learned more than I could imagine about my profession and my daughter was able to have an amazing international experience at a very young age."

Picking an organization that supports balance is a key first step. It probably isn't something to bring up in your interview, but it is something to ask about through your network. Set real boundaries at work so you can have a healthy home life. If you consistently have conflicts between work and home, maybe it's time to find a new organization that is a better fit.

Hire a wife

Trista got some eye-opening advice when she asked her friend Athena Adkins, nonprofit rockstar and supermom, how she does it all. Athena said that the only way that she had seen a woman with children succeed at the top levels of an organization — without a stay-at-home husband — was when women hired a "wife." Trista had never heard of hiring a wife (outside of the occasional mail-order bride news story), so she was confused. What Athena meant was hiring someone who handles the worry and responsibility of managing your home.

Trista says, "Initially I got pretty ticked off. How unfair is it that men just go off to work and don't worry about keeping their home life running smoothly? Is this just another case of the rich getting richer because they can afford to hire the help that allows them to achieve more at work? Then I realized that I was relieved to find out that there weren't these magical women out there effortlessly hosting a dinner party for 15 after successfully managing a difficult merger at work."

Here's how to spread the wifely duties around:

Negotiate up front with your partner about who does what

Trista spent many years of her marriage assuming that her husband understood that a laundry basket next to the stairs meant that he should bring the basket downstairs and start the laundry. Recently, however, she has tried to stop assuming he is a mind reader and actually asks when she wants something done.

Teach children to be responsible for themselves

There is a great book called *Parenting with Love and Logic* that says only one person can really worry about a problem. If you spend time worrying about your child completing a homework assignment, they won't worry about it because they know you have it covered and will nag them at the appropriate time. Letting kids be responsible for their own stuff is great practice for the rest of their lives and relieves you of a ton of stress.

Buy time

Arguing about household duties that could easily be hired out is a waste of precious family time. There are grocery delivery services, meal assembly stores, and a ton of people that offer housecleaning and yard care on the popular community site Craigslist.org. Figure out what things make financial and mental health sense to outsource, and try them out for yourself.

Nonprofit Rockstar: Robyn Schein

Robyn Schein, a philanthropic advisor at the Minneapolis Foundation, is a great example of someone who has been very thoughtful about how to balance home and work. Robyn says:

"A few years ago my husband and I knew we were ready to start a family, but I was also committed to my work. I was working in philanthropy, which was always a goal. I had responsibility and I was working on projects I really cared about. Work was a clear priority. Did I really want to complicate that?

I spoke with a lot of women at all stages of their careers that were also moms and asked about work-life balance. From those conversations I realized that work-life balance would be an ongoing challenge — regardless of when or how many kids I had. I was most nervous about taking maternity leave and what that would mean for my projects and my career path. Would it take me out of the game? Would it slow the progress I had worked so hard for?

I have now had two children (in 2 years!) and have taken three months off each time. I believe that each experience has actually helped me professionally. I returned from both maternity leaves with renewed focus. The time away allowed me to see things more strategically. As I was catching up with co-workers, I listened carefully to the status of their work. The opportunity to listen helped me to evaluate where my work aligned, [as well as] opportunities for collaboration and streamlined processes.

However, the most dramatic change was the chance to let go of bad habits and start new, more efficient behaviors. I have an amazing family waiting for me at home at the end of the day. The more directed and efficient I am during the day, the more quality time I will be able to spend with my kids.

Now truthfully, between those days when all the stars align and I feel like I've excelled at work and home, there are certainly days when everything feels out of whack. I remind myself that tomorrow is another day and in the big scheme of life I am fortunate to have my family and a fulfilling, productive career!"

Chapter 7: Move On Up

Now that you've figured out some ways to plan for balance in your current nonprofit role, it may be easier to imagine ways to accelerate your career. In this chapter, we offer several concrete tips for moving on up the nonprofit career ladder.

Tip 37: Create Your Own Professional Development Plan

Every once in a while, you'll see an amazing fellowship program that makes you dream about uninterrupted months exploring your vocation, interviewing experts from around the world, and sipping tea in a retreat center in the hills of Italy as you plan your next 10 years. While it is wonderful to participate in an organized fellowship, you don't have to wait until you are accepted to have a similar experience. Here are some things that you can do on your own to develop the fellowship of your dreams:

- Hire an executive coach
- Take a career interest inventory or personality tests
- Interview experts in your field (locally, nationally, or internationally)
- Present at a conference
- Get mentored by a seasoned leader
- Attend conferences of your choosing
- Do a leadership project
- Take classes on topic of your choice

- Take time for reflection

- Write a final paper or blog posts about your experience

- Purchase professional development materials or workbooks

You can also apply for a traditional fellowship. See the resources section in the back of the book for a list of Foundation and Nonprofit Fellowships to check out.

Tip 38: Set Big Goals

Sometimes it's too scary to decide what your big, hairy, audacious goals are because you are worried about possible disappointment. It's easy to stay in your cubicle, keep your head down, and keep working. When you do that, the chances of failure are pretty low.

But the problem with settling for average is that you don't really get away from that possible disappointment; you just get that disappointment in little chunks, day by day. Big disappointment is not getting the job that you interviewed for that you thought was a perfect fit. Little disappointment is seeing your co-workers move up in your organization and you staying in place because you were too afraid to try. Little disappointment is seeing that your college roommate just became the board chair of that wonderful civic organization that you love, while you were too nervous to volunteer to help with their annual event.

The first step to getting out of the rut of thinking small is to think BIG. Thinking big is figuring out what you would like to be doing twenty years from now and taking the first step now to get there. Here are some steps to take:

Figure out what the target is

Brainstorm what your big, hairy, audacious, completely-out-of-your-league goal is. Make the goal so exciting that you can't wait to start working on it.

Break it into manageable pieces

Most big goals feel completely overwhelming when you look at them. You may be thinking, "I can hardly find the time to set up my LinkedIn profile. How am I going to be able to do what it takes to become the head of a youth development organization?" Break the goal into yearly, monthly, and weekly chunks. Brainstorm as many of the steps that you can think of to get to the larger goal.

For example:

10 Year Goal: Become President of a Youth Development Organization

In the next five years:

- Obtain MBA with a focus on social entrepreneurism
- Become a visible speaker on youth development
- Expand network to include board members of youth-serving organizations

In the next year:

- Research top MBA programs with social entrepreneurism focus
- Apply to four of those programs
- Start a blog on trends in youth development
- Set up six informational interviews with youth development staff members

In the next week:

- Set up a Google Alert for youth development news stories
- Ask your mentor for business school recommendations
- Buy a domain name for your blog

- Join Toastmasters to improve your public speaking skills

Setting small, manageable goals with the big picture in mind helps you more quickly reach your goals.

Talk about it

Telling people in your network what your long-term ambitions are will open up resources and connections that you didn't know existed. Your friends and colleagues are nearly limitless sources of information and expertise that are only available if you let them know what your grand plan is.

Trista told members of her philanthropy network that her long-term goal was to run a foundation. She had expected it to be a 10-year goal. But because she was preparing and people knew what she wanted, when her dream position came open, members of her network forwarded her the announcement and encouraged her to apply. They also served as her recommenders and said good things about her to the foundation's board of directors.

Make it part of your professional development plan

There are opportunities to work towards your long-term goals within your current position. Your relationship with your supervisor and their willingness to support your long term growth will determine how much of your long-term plan you can feel comfortable sharing.

David Nicholson, a program director at the Headwaters Foundation for Justice, shared that his 10-year goal was to run international giving circles. While his foundation has a local focus, there is great need for the organization to develop a scalable model for giving circles. Trista tasked him with developing that model for the foundation. This helps him get closer to his dream, while adding real value to his organization.

Nonprofit Rockstar: Ben Jealous

Ben Jealous is the definition of nonprofit rockstar who has achieved his big, hairy, audacious goal. At the age of 35, he was selected as the president of the nation's oldest civil rights organization, the National Association for the Advancement of Colored People (NAACP). He is the youngest president in the organization's history.

Ben may be young, but he has a lifetime of experience that has prepared him for this position. He organized a voter registration drive at age 14. As a college student he worked for the NAACP Legal Defense and Educational Fund in Harlem as a community organizer. He then received a Rhodes Scholarship and studied at Oxford. He was a community organizer and served as a reporter and managing editor for the Jackson Advocate in Mississippi. Later, he directed the U.S. Human Rights Program of Amnesty International in Washington, D.C. Most recently he was president of the Rosenberg Foundation. Marian Wright Edelman of the Children's Defense Fund said of Ben's appointment, "I hope many young people will be inspired by this new leader and pledge their support for the challenges ahead."

Tip 39: Get a Master's Degree

Rosetta figured out where she wanted to be early on — the nonprofit sector. Unfortunately, she also realized early on that nonprofit work can pretty much suck if you have to be a receptionist or an administrative assistant for the first five years of your career, and she was determined not to have to do that.

So, when Rosetta stepped off the stage as a new college graduate years ago, she also knew that the next step for her would be graduate school. She quickly chose a graduate degree program in the city she wanted to work in (DC) and began her first real nonprofit job at the same time. She ended up selecting Trinity Washington University's master's program for the most part because the program could be completed in an accelerated time frame (half the time of a traditional master's), and she was both impatient and an overachiever. The coursework wasn't too shabby either:

- ADMN 601 Excellence in Managing Contemporary Organizations

- ADMN 603 Theories of Leadership and Organizational Change
- ADMN 605 Group Dynamics and Team Building
- ADMN 607 Financial Management for Non-Financial Managers
- ADMN 609 Introduction to Research
- ADMN 677 Effective Human Resource Strategies
- ADMN 631 Trends and Issues in Nonprofit Management
- ADMN 633 Nonprofit Marketing and Public Relations
- ADMN 635 Government Relations and Grant Writing
- ADMN 637 Resource Development and Fundraising
- ADMN 638 Financial Management and Budgeting
- ADMN 639 Nonprofit Strategic Planning and Board Development

Most nonprofit workers will tell you that you do not need an advanced degree to succeed in a nonprofit career, and we would agree with them in a general sense. For the kinds of entry-level positions in which college graduates are usually placed, a rapid typing speed, can-do attitude, and a strong sense of patience are all you need to do data entry, answer phones, make endless copies, or stuff envelopes. But if you want to move up in the sector more quickly and actually make a living wage from doing the work of social change, you may want to consider pursuing a master's degree. Perhaps this is becoming more and more true for all professions, but it is certainly a trend in the nonprofit sector.

Rosetta began her full-time nonprofit career as an administrative assistant, then graduated to a program assistant, and then a director of development, all within different organizations and subsectors and all within three years, doubling her salary in that same timeframe. She learned a lot in all of her positions, and was clearly competent before she went to graduate school, but try telling that to the folks she interviewed with as she kept trying to apply her skills to more advanced positions. All they could see was that she hadn't "put in her time" long enough to know anything.

For that reason alone, Rosetta is sure that she would not have been able to land a director of development position if not for her master's degree in Nonprofit Management. Trinity University taught Rosetta well and gave her a strong foundation with which to make sense out of her experience, but it also gave her something that her few years of experience could not: credibility. The first thing Rosetta's last boss said as he introduced her to the board chair in her first week of work was, "Meet Rosetta Thurman. She has a master's degree." Smiles all around.

Trista knew that a master's degree was essential for her to get a senior-level position in the social sector. Because she was clear about her career path, a master's in Public Policy was an easy choice. Because she had been working in nonprofit organizations since she was 14, she felt very comfortable going straight to graduate school after receiving her bachelor's degree. Trista's advice if you are considering a switch into the nonprofit sector is to get some hands-on experience before getting a degree. The class work will make more sense and then you will be more sure that the sector is a fit for your skills and expertise.

Rosetta and Trista's experiences are similar to many stories we have heard from nonprofit professionals trying to break into upper management. Sometimes, to get past the barriers facing promotion, we need to take matters into our own hands. It was well worth it to us to obtain our master's degrees. Don't think you have to "put in your time" just because that's how everyone else has done it.

How to choose a master's program

Heather Carpenter – practitioner, scholar, blogger, and all-around nonprofit rockstar – says, "there is a lot of confusion about nonprofit-focused master's degree programs. There are many different types of master's degree programs that can be considered nonprofit-focused or nonprofit education." On her blog, Heather offers a list of these types, including:

- Master's of Nonprofit Administration
- Master's of Public Administration
- Master's of Social Work

- Master's of Business Administration

- Master's of Public Policy

- Master's of Human Services

- Master's of Arts in Philanthropic Studies

If you are interested in becoming an Executive Director of a nonprofit, then you should consider pursuing a stand-alone **Master's of Nonprofit Administration** (aka MNO/MNS/MNM/MS in NP). These master's degree programs offer core and elective courses in managing a nonprofit organization. These courses include: Nonprofit Management, Board Governance, Fundraising, Nonprofit Finance and Accounting, Capital Campaign and Development, Strategic Planning, Human Resources, etc.

If you are interested in studying the intersection between government and nonprofits, then you should consider pursuing a **Master's of Public Administration** (a.k.a MPSA, MPIA) with a Specialization in Nonprofit Management. These master's degree programs offer core courses in managing a governmental organization and offer elective courses in managing a nonprofit organization. Also some of these programs focus on NGO's (international nonprofit organizations).

If you are interested in becoming a nonprofit board member (or nonprofit manager) and studying earned revenue within nonprofits, then you should consider pursuing a **Master's of Business Administration** with a specialization in Nonprofit Management. These master's degree programs offer core courses in managing a business and offer elective courses in managing a nonprofit organization.

If you are interested in directly working with clients and constituents on a daily basis and managing the programmatic side of nonprofit organizations, then you should consider pursuing a **Master's of Social Work** with a specialization in Nonprofit Management. These master's degree programs offer core courses in social welfare and social change and offer elective courses in managing a nonprofit organization.

If you are interested in changing social policy related to nonprofit organizations, then you should consider pursuing a **Master's of Public Policy** (a.k.a. MA in PP, MPPA) with a specialization in Nonprofit Management. These master's degree programs offer core courses in creating and changing public policy and offer elective courses in managing a nonprofit organization.

If you are interested in directly running human service organizations, then you should consider pursuing a **Master's of Science in Human Services**. These master's degree programs offer core and elective courses in managing human and social services organizations.

Finally, if you are interested in studying philanthropic giving within nonprofit organizations, then you should consider pursuing a **Masters of Arts in Philanthropic Studies.** This master's degree program offers core and elective courses in philanthropic giving within nonprofit organizations and the sector.

Remember, these descriptions above are generalizations. You should ALWAYS visit a master's degree program website to see the specific courses offered within the program.

Tip 40: Manage Up

If your supervisor is successful, it is more likely that you will be successful in your position. And the best way to ensure your supervisor's success is to lighten their load. This means going above and beyond your job description by assisting your boss with their core tasks. Here are some ways to do that:

Know your boss's headaches

If you understand the pressure and constraints that your boss faces, you are less likely to add pressure in those areas. You will also develop a more empathetic perspective of the pressures of leadership.

Take something off his/her plate

A good habit is to consistently ask your supervisor, "Is there something that I can help you with?" Also, listen to how your supervisor describes current projects. You'll hear which ones are extra stressful and which ones are critical for the organization's success. Remember that the first way you can take something off his/her plate is to do a good job with your current responsibilities.

Bring solutions, not problems

Mary Lee Hoffman, the former CEO of a Minnesota Girl Scout council, used to say, "I am always available to talk with you about an organizational issue. I'll even take you to lunch when we talk about it, but you have to have 2-3 solutions to the problem already thought out before you set the appointment."

This culture of focusing on solutions encouraged staff members to act as problem solvers, not just complainers. Develop this practice when you interact with your boss.

Use their time wisely

Don't come to your boss with every little problem. Keep a running list of topics that you need to talk about with your supervisor and hold it until your next meeting. Also spend some time preparing for those meetings so you both get the most out of that time together.

Be a truth teller

It sometimes feels like it's only the "yes men" who get ahead. But the truth is that these people can really only get so far because when you are surrounded by people that are only telling you what they think you want to hear, you don't ever hear what you *need* to hear. Be known as someone who can be depended on for the truth about a situation. Truthfulness and diplomacy about how you deliver that truth will turn you into a trusted advisor and will serve your organization well.

Have their back

When you represent your supervisor well and keep their and the organization's best interests front and center, they are more likely to let you represent them internally and externally. It's also important that you and your supervisor stay on the same team, even when you disagree. Colin Powell, former U.S. Secretary of State and nonprofit board member extraordinaire, said "When we are debating an issue, loyalty means giving me your honest opinion, whether you think I'll like it or not. Disagreement, at this stage, stimulates me. But once a decision has been made, the debate ends. From that point on loyalty means executing the decision as if it were your own."

Some of you may be thinking, "I can see how these tips could be helpful if my boss is a great leader, but my boss is an idiot." But managing up is not just about getting the most out of an effective leader, it is also about making difficult supervisors more tolerable. You may find that your boss is doing a bad job because he is completely overwhelmed by his responsibilities, or maybe she treats you badly because she feels like you don't have her back. Before placing all of the blame on your supervisor, first figure out if there is more that you could be doing to manage up.

Who gets the credit?

Sometimes the problem isn't that you aren't lightening your manager's load; it's that you are handling many of your supervisor's responsibilities and not getting any credit for doing so, or maybe it's that you came up with a wonderful idea for your organization and it was passed off as someone else's idea. This is very touchy territory. Sometime you have to be OK with letting go of some credit. It would be great if your boss always told people about the contribution you made to a specific project. That doesn't always happen. Sometimes it's as simple as someone forgetting to properly thank you. Sometimes they have forgotten the work that you did early in a project if they then took over a project and ran with it. Or sometimes it's because they are an evil jerk/genius that is trying to take all of the credit and leave you in the dust. Regardless of the reason, this is really a no-win situation, because if you raise a fuss you look like a diva, a liar, or a credit seeker, none of which are pretty.

Finally, be sure to document the work that you have been doing, so that during review time you have a record of your accomplishments. If giving proper credit continues to be a problem, we recommend finding another organization that will appreciate your hard work.

Tip 41: Get Paid What You Are Worth

In an interview with the Zora & Alice blog, Thalia Theodore Washington, the Executive Director of DonorsChoose.org, talks about her experience negotiating her salary.

"My second job was in a nonprofit in LA. I'll tell the end of the story first, which is that I didn't negotiate and I should have. I was young, it was my first office job, and I had no idea what I was worth.

I still to this day kick myself for not negotiating. And the reason is that you're always building off of your last salary. You don't have a $30,000 salary and then your next job's $100,000. There are stages.

The fear I had and the fear that women have is that negotiating makes you seem greedy, not classy; it's a knock against your integrity. Yet, now that I have had the chance to hire people, I would argue that there's something to be said for advocating for yourself. Probably everyone has a job where an offer was made and you just said yes. But smart people don't always just say yes."

Here are some ways to negotiate a higher starting salary:

Look at salary surveys

These surveys can give you an idea of what local positions, in similar size organizations are paying. Many organizations use these salary surveys to set their salary scales within the organization. Your local nonprofit association may produce a salary survey, or you can look at Idealist's listing of surveys at http://www.idealist.org/en/career/salarysurveys.html.   Use these numbers when you are considering positions at a variety of organizations (e.g. larger organizations often offer a higher salary) and to give you an idea of what to expect during salary negotiations.

Check out the 990

We told you that salary often is dependent on an organization's operating budget, and the place to find that number is on the 990. The 990 is a document required by the IRS for tax-exempt organizations. This form will give you an idea of how large the organization's budget is and tell you how much the top paid staff at the organization are paid (if their salary is over $50,000 a year). Even if the position that you are interested in is not listed on the 990, you can determine what their salary scale looks like compared to similar sized organizations by looking at what they pay their top staff. You can find 990s at www.guidestar.org.

Be truthful but don't overshare

Don't ever lie about your salary history. The HR department will check your salary history and being a liar isn't going to help your career. Instead of listing salary history on an application, list your desired salary range for the current position.

Just say "hmm"

Most people immediately accept the first offer from an employer. Even a reflective "okay" when they say the first salary number can immediately end negotiation. Pausing for a second and saying "hmm" or "that's a little lower than I expected" opens the door for negotiation. The hiring manager almost always has flexibility and starts with a lowball number to leave room to negotiate. So remember, that uncomfortable two minutes could mean thousands of extra dollars in your pocket over time.

Many people worry that negotiating makes you look greedy. That is not the case, even in nonprofits. You want the hiring manager to know that you are a valuable asset to the organization and whatever the final number is, that you were a steal.

You can use similar strategies for negotiating a raise:

Ask for a review

Don't be afraid to ask for a review and a compensation conversation (make sure timing is before budgeting begins). Be prepared for this conversation with a document that outlines your responsibilities and accomplishments. You should keep a folder with emails of people thanking you when you do well and a list of projects and results. If your boss can't give you the full raise that you think that you deserve and know is in the budget, ask for another review in six months to reevaluate your work.

Erica, a program associate at a youth services agency, shares her experience:

"After my first salary discussion, I cried in the bathroom because I thought my boss understood that I was doing a great job and would give me the 10% increase that I expected (based on pay in similar organizations). Since she was not a mind reader, she gave me the 2% cost of living increase that everyone else got. I got it together and told her my concerns that I was being underpaid for the level of work that I was doing and was offered a promotion with a salary increase larger than the 10% that I was hoping for."

Get a friend on the inside

Find someone within your organization (in HR or another manager besides your boss) that can tell you the real range of the raise that your boss is able to give you. Having this number in your back pocket will prepare you to give a realistic counter-offer when your boss gives a number for your raise.

Know the culture

Know the compensation culture at your organization (some *only* do cost of living increases and some *only* grant raises when your title changes). Know how many title changes are available in your current position and the average raise for each move (e.g. associate, officer, director). Develop a timeline for when you would like to make these moves and be clear with your supervisor that you are interested in moving up.

Don't settle for pauper's wages because you are subsidizing the work of your organization. Go someplace where you are paid for the skills that you bring to the organization. And if you really want to support the work of a particular organization, you might want to do it through charitable gifts rather than a crappy salary.

Tip 42: Consider the Benefits

You: a brilliant, energetic young professional who wants to make a difference in the world. What you're looking for: a nonprofit job that can turn into a fulfilling career with a salary that doesn't put you into the poorhouse. If you're reading this, chances are you already know where to find a nonprofit job. The problem is that you may not know what to look for once you apply for the job and start the process of determining whether you want to take the job or not.

Here's the thing: Being satisfied with your salary, while important, is just one factor.

Even though you may be offered a great salary, you may end up with crappy benefits or a toxic workplace. You may find a job you're really excited about, but at the end of the day, no matter what the mission, or how much you may like your co-workers, you have to make sure the job will be beneficial to your long-term career goals and personal well-being. If you dive in headfirst without thinking it through, you could end up hating your nonprofit job.

Here are five factors (beyond salary) that you might consider in a nonprofit job. Your goal should be to negotiate the ones that mean the most to you into your offer before you accept a position.

- **Generous vacation time:** This means at least four weeks off a year. Your work will, at times, be very difficult and you will need a break. A long one. More than just two weeks once a year. Make sure you have enough time allocated so that you can enjoy your time off. If you're offered only two weeks, ask for four as part of a counter offer, especially if the salary is not ideal.

- **Fully paid health benefits:** This means health, dental, and vision covered by the organization. You don't want to worry about how your doctor bills are going to get paid. Rosetta once met a young woman who worked in an arts organization that refused to provide her with even basic coverage. The young woman was broke, miserable, and resented her job every time she got sick and had to pay out of pocket. It was really a lose-lose situation for everyone.

- **Flexible scheduling:** You want to have the option to switch up your hours when you need to, work from home periodically, or take on a slash career. What if you need to leave at 3 p.m. to pick up your sick kid? You don't want to work in a place that frowns upon work/life balance, even if that means you need to come into work on Tuesdays at 10 a.m. because you have a personal trainer or do yoga in the morning.

- **403(b) retirement account:** This refers to an employer plan set up to allow you to save for retirement. It's best if the organization offers some kind of match in addition to your contributions. It makes your money grow faster! And knowing that your nonprofit cares about your long-term financial future will only make you more loyal to the organization.

- **Professional development opportunities:** Ideally, there would a set amount in the budget for staff to attend conferences or workshops to hone their skills.

But, in these tough economic times, many nonprofits will tell you that they've cut their professional development budgets. Ask anyway. And if there's an annual conference you really want to attend, work the cost into your salary negotiations. You can also sweeten the deal by offering to come back to the office and train all the other staff on what you learned at a particular workshop.

In our nonprofit careers, we've learned that everything is negotiable. Everything. Especially if you can prove that you have the kind of exceptional talent that the organization needs to succeed. If you have a stellar personal brand and can prove that you'll be a great asset to the organization, the door will be open to getting the best benefits to accompany your salary. In the end, it's all about what's important to YOU.

Tip 43: Get Promoted

Six months into her new position as a development associate at a small youth development organization, Dana realized that she was really doing the work of a development director. She was in her early 20s just starting out in her career. Yet Dana's job duties had become more and more complex, and while she enjoyed all the different aspects of fundraising, she felt that her title and salary should change due to the advanced nature of her work.

In just six months, Dana had implemented their first online giving program, engaged new donors, and successfully organized a large fundraising event that brought in thousands of dollars. When she came to the executive director to ask for a raise and a title change to Development Director, her boss was all too happy to oblige. After all, they certainly didn't want to lose Dana, a valuable employee with proven results.

Sound like a Cinderella story? Well, it's not. It's true, and Dana shows that young nonprofit professionals *can* get promoted very quickly in an organization if they play their cards right.

Ask for a title change

Especially if you work for a small nonprofit, where job descriptions and titles can be fluid, you can buck the system and get promoted "in title," as they say. If you find yourself with managerial duties on your plate, while working with the title of "assistant," it may be time to have a conversation with your boss about what's possible. We suggest requesting a 30-minute meeting with your supervisor (don't make too big of a deal about it) and explain how your job description is really equivalent to that of a "manager" or "director" title. It also helps to have a few job descriptions from other nonprofits handy to prove your point. You may not get a raise to go along with it, but future employers will always offer you more money if you have 'manager' or 'director' on your resume quicker than they will if all you have is a history of being an 'assistant.'

Do your job really well

The first year of a nonprofit job is critical. Don't be a slacker. Come in to work on time and do an excellent job within the position you were hired for. If you are in charge of a program or project, make sure it doesn't just get done, but do it in a remarkable way, on time and within budget. Instead of coming to work just to "do your job," try to exceed the goals that the organization has for you or your department. If you need to raise $100,000, raise $150,000. If you're tasked with recruiting 20 mentors, go out and find 25. While you'll still get a paycheck, doing the bare minimum is not going to be enough to get you promoted to a job with more responsibility and/or more pay. Doing your job well means going the extra mile when your colleagues need help, too.

Become a rainmaker

A rainmaker is someone who has a knack for using their connections to benefit their company with new clients, customers, or investors. When you come into a new nonprofit job, don't be afraid to use your personal networks to connect you to opportunities that will benefit the organization. If you belong to an alumni association, ask your fellow classmates to volunteer or donate to your cause. Put messages out on your Facebook and Twitter profiles to increase attendance at your nonprofit's events. Help garner press for your agency by calling in a favor from your friend who works at a local newspaper. If you can bring in new assets that the nonprofit didn't have before they hired you, your name will be at the top of the list when an internal leadership position opens up.

Dana was promoted within six months because she did a great job, brought in new assets, and then *asked* to be promoted. While it's easy to get comfortable in your job, you really have to stay at the top of your game if you want to move up in your career in your current organization or otherwise.

Tip 44: Introduce Yourself to a Search Firm

A search firm is an organization that is hired by a nonprofit to fill a specific position, usually more senior positions (director, vice president, and executive director searches are common). Search firms are paid fees to perform this service. Sometimes the fees are contingent on the person hired staying at the organization for a set amount of time, so search firms have a large incentive to make sure that the people that they recruit are a strong fit for the organization's needs and culture. So how do you help search consultants find you?

Have a strong professional network

Most search consultants find their candidates through referrals in their network. Follow the suggestions in Chapter 4 to build your own network and increase your chances to be referred to an executive search firm. If you are called by a search consultant and the position is not a good fit for you, return the networking favor and suggest 3-5 people from your own network who might be a fit for the position.

Identify the right firms

Most search firms have a specific niche, like healthcare nonprofits, large social service agencies, or Midwest foundations. Identify these foundations with Google searches and by noticing who is referenced as the search consultant in position descriptions that you are interested in. Learn more about that firm from their website and set up informational interviews with search consultant at those firms.

Send a resume that highlights your skills

Even if the firm isn't doing a search right now that would be a fit for you, they often have databases where they will enter your information for future searches. Make sure that you highlight your skills both in the resume and in the cover letter.

Ask a recruiter

Vincent Robinson, the founder of the search firm The 360 Group, answers some of the common questions that nonprofit professionals have for search firms but are afraid to ask.

How is working with a search firm different than working directly with the nonprofit?

There are actually quite a few differences, but the key difference for candidates to remember is that the search firm has the organization as its client. Search firms have a strong interest in making the right match. Certainly everyone does in hiring matters, but as third-party participants, it is incumbent upon firms to learn as much as they can about the client organization and develop insights about the organization that those on the inside may not be able to see quite as clearly. The search firm, then, is much more than a gatekeeper, as candidates sometimes think — someone to get around, rather that someone from whom to learn about the client organization. Search consultancies are also "on point" to manage all aspects of a search. While client organizations appreciate the deep insight on the role, the organization, and the candidates that outstanding consultants provide, they also appreciate firms' taking on the search from start to finish, precisely because they do not want to interact directly with the entire pool of candidates, creating value for the client on both sides of the impending transaction.Finally, at their best, search firms can help candidates better prepare for their interviews and other interactions with the client — they know the issues that are foremost in clients' minds. However, it is important to note that search consultants (and their staffs) are watching candidates' behavior both "on-stage" (in interviews) and "off-stage" (more casual settings or interacting with administrative staff). This is something that a hiring organization cannot do nearly as fully as a dedicated, outside consultant.

Should I contact you if I am interested in a position or should I just send in my resume?

This varies widely. The best thing to do is take the lead from the firms themselves. As a small, boutique consultancy, for example, our firm has very limited capacity to speak with every candidate in a given role. The wisest method for expressing interest in a position is to read the position description very carefully, and develop a cover letter and resume that reflects a candidate's best thinking about how their skills and experience could fulfill the position responsibilities *as indicated in the position description.*

We often see candidates vying for leadership positions missing this mark, because they already know what a president or CEO does; the firm has taken great care to express what the role *actually* is and what the organization *actually* wants. Because organizations differ from each other and over time, a president is not a president is not a president.

Our firm is, and has been from its start, deeply committed to promoting diversity of all sorts in leadership in the social sector. As a result, we are quite open-minded to candidates whom we do not already know. In fact, we welcome the opportunity to meet and get acquainted with the rich breadth of people who make up this sector. The best way for us to start and develop our acquaintance, however, is through an application for a specific role. If we spoke to every candidate who wanted to get to know us, we would not have any time to complete our searches and deepen our relationships with our clients and the sector at large. That's why, among many other reasons, that if a candidate is truly interested in a position, they should *apply*. Don't overthink the process or play games; review all available materials, write a thoughtful cover letter, and customize your resume to highlight particular areas of strength vis-a-vis the position under consideration.

I want to apply for an executive director position, but I'm afraid that I'm too young for the position. Will you laugh at me if I send in an application?

Ha! I'm laughing already. I'm laughing because, as I just said, organizations have different leadership needs at different points in time. I think it's really important for all candidates to reflect on their skills, their aspirations, and the contributions they can make to an organization as they develop their application materials. I repeat: skills, aspirations, and contributions. The truth is, more often than not, younger people think more about their aspirations than the others. I became an executive director at age 31. While I loved that job, only nearly ten years later do I have a deeper appreciation for the skills I have to offer organizations. This just takes time — but for the more self-reflective of us, it doesn't have to take all that long. People just need more experience under their belts and the inclination to contemplate where they fit — to themselves, and with others.

A friend of mine, roughly my age, went from running a local organization to a national organization. He told me recently that even he thought that might have been a stretch. A couple of board members knew him, and were able to persuade their colleagues to have a closer look (this can also be a role of an excellent search consultant). Had he doubted that he would have been taken seriously, he wouldn't have the position that he has, in which he is wildly successful, and I know his board is very pleased with the prominence he has brought the organization. Wouldn't his selecting out have been a shame? The worst that can happen to you is that you can be told "no." And the best? Well, I've just given you a couple of examples. So think about what you bring, and what you want to give, ask for advice along the way, and your aspirations have a much better chance of being realized.

The organization that I am interested in applying for says they are interested in diverse candidates, but I know their organization and it's not diverse at all. As a person of color, do I really have a shot or do they just say they want diversity because it looks good?

This is a great question, and one that reflects our 21st-century society. These issues remain challenging ones to tackle, but as our society is becoming much more diverse at every level of educational attainment and professional success, they are certainly more of a consideration for organizations than they have been in a long time. (The 1980s stunted the previous decades' progress on this, but that is only my humble opinion.)

At this point, many organizations in our sector do want more diverse perspectives to push the thinking about impact well beyond where it has been. There are certainly some organizations that challenge the notion that more diversity can lead to richer outcomes, but they are becoming a, ahem, minority of organizations.

That said, and this gets to the core of your question, don't assume that you know where they are on the "diversity-o-meter." Just because an organization does not look diverse does not mean that it fully intends to become more diverse. Similarly, the dint of diversity may belie attitudes within. I was once visiting with the human resources director at an organization who told me that the group really, really wanted more diversity — and that they were willing to sacrifice on quality to achieve that goal.

I want to talk about "diverse," though. Strictly speaking, a person is not "diverse." A group is, an organization can be, but a person is not "diverse." A person has diverse interests, skills, and friends, perhaps, but no one person on her or his own is diverse. A great search consultant is not afraid to discuss these issues head-on with their clients, nor should they be reluctant to discuss it with candidates. It is a perfectly fair question for a candidate to ask about an organization's desires for diversity. And the candidate should trust a search consultant's opinion, unless there are reasons not to do so. Great consultants, though, will tell you the truth, because ultimately, they want the organization to be happy, the candidate to be successful, and the union of the two to be powerful.

The art of the phone interview

Commongood Careers, a fabulous search firm that works exclusively with nonprofits and social innovators, has great advice on how to interact with search consultants during the hiring process. You can find a wealth of articles and advice, as well as job listings at some of the nation's most exciting organizations, on their website www.cgcareers.org. Here is their advice on managing the phone interview, a common part of working with a search firm.

Phone interviews present the unique challenge of communicating your enthusiasm and relevant experiences without the benefits of eye contact, body language, dressing to impress, and a hearty handshake. However, the phone interview is often a critical part of the hiring process that will determine the fate of your candidacy. The following article walks you through the phases of the phone interview and shares a collection of insider tips that can help propel you to the next stages of the interview process.

Before the interview

Acknowledge the importance of the phone interview. Being invited to a phone interview does not mean that you are not good enough for an in-person interview. Because nonprofits are often stretched for time, many organizations have adopted the phone interview as the initial stage of the process.

Respect the scheduling process. Treat all pre-interview communications with your interviewer as opportunities to demonstrate your competency and decorum. Following directions is extremely important and will show your interviewer that you respect their processes. Also, make yourself available during normal work hours. Asking an interviewer to be available at 9 p.m. for an interview will translate as being disrespectful of the interviewer's personal life. If the interviewer explains that the conversation should last 20-30 minutes, be prepared to tailor your answers to fit within that time slot. Simple considerations and following directions demonstrates to the interviewer that you pay attention to details and are considerate of the hiring process.

Research the organization and the position. In the week(s) before your interview, visit the organization's website and search the web for articles to gain an understanding of the nonprofit's programs and learn about its history. Additionally, read the job description closely and prepare questions if you need components of the job description better explained. Prepare bullet points that explain a specific example of a time that you fulfilled a qualification required for the role. Citing specific examples from your previous work experience will make your phone interview more memorable for the interviewer.

Prepare thoughtful questions and a final statement in advance. As a candidate, you can always expect the phone interview to conclude with the interviewer asking if you have any final questions. Asking thoughtful questions at the end of an interview gives the interviewee an opportunity to show some critical thinking skills. However, coming up with thoughtful questions during an interview can be extremely difficult, so prepare your queries before the call.

Additionally, prepare in advance a quick ten-second personal pitch for why you are the right person for the job. Doing so will help you clarify your motives for applying and will put you in a confident frame of mind for the interview.

During the call

Be enthusiastic. A great way to nail the first impression is to sound happy, friendly, and enthusiastic about the conversation. Communicating excitement for the opportunity will demonstrate to the interviewer that you are someone who has passion and optimism. A tactic to naturally sound more enthusiastic is to stand during the phone call. Standing up allows more oxygen to flow through your airways, making your voice sound more energized and robust.

Remember that your interviewer is taking notes. As you speak, your interviewer is most likely taking notes. S/he will need some record of the conversation either for his/her recollection or to be able to effectively share your candidacy with other members of the staff. Speak clearly and at a reasonable pace.

Stay focused. As you are asked questions, jot the question down. Tell your interviewer that you are going to do this, so s/he does not think you are pausing to do something unrelated to the interview. Writing the question will help to keep your answer focused and concise. If you are starting to stray off topic, being able to visualize the question can help you stay on topic. If you need more time to answer the question, request some time to reflect so you can give the best answer.

Communicate a balance of passion and experience. The interviewer wants to hear that you are passionate about the mission of the organization, but s/he also wants to hear examples of how you have demonstrated your passion in past experiences. Providing a philosophical/ethical foundation for why you want to work for the mission is also vital to the success of the phone interview.

Be honest about your salary requirements. If the conversation turns to the topic of salary, be honest about your requirements for the role. If the interviewer shares the expected range, it is most likely the case that the range will not drastically change during the hiring process. Deflating your requirements so that you are moved forward in the process will result in wasted time and will reflect poorly on you as a job seeker. Therefore, if it is impossible for you to accept the stated salary range, take yourself out of consideration and keep looking for other opportunities.

The phone interview can make the difference between moving ahead in the hiring process or checking your candidacy at the door. With careful preparation and a positive attitude, you can sail through the phone interview and emerge as a strong candidate for the role.

Tip 45: Use Your Network to Find a New Job

If you are seeking out a new nonprofit job, you may not want your colleagues at your current job to know. It can be difficult to find new opportunities without letting your boss know that you're looking. But if you're not ready to have a frank conversation with your boss, don't let that keep you from finding a great new nonprofit job! Using a combination of your existing network and online tools, you can tap into new job opportunities while you still have the security of your current job. Here's how:

Post a good profile

Posting your resume online can bring you unexpected opportunities. Take some time and post an overview of your work experience and skills on sites like LinkedIn and Visual CV. Be brief, but detailed in describing your previous positions, education and training, and skills you'd like to use in your next job. Don't forget to mention any relevant awards you've received or professional associations you're affiliated with. Also consider posting a photo of yourself along with your resume so that potential employers can see your smiling face as someone they would love to work with.

Browse new opportunities

Don't be afraid to browse for new jobs that might interest you. It may take you six months to a year to find something that's just right for you, so don't rush it by jumping on the first thing that sounds interesting. Set up alerts on nonprofit job sites that will deliver results to you every week. Take your time and apply only if the job sounds like a good fit. You don't have to tell your boss about any interviews you have unless you've received an offer from another organization and you're ready to leave your current job.

Use email as a discreet networking tool

If you don't want to announce to the whole world that you're looking for a new nonprofit gig, it's best to contact a group of select colleagues via email. You should definitely use your work contacts (excluding your boss) as resources for your job search. Let them know that you're exploring new career opportunities and you would love their help if they come across any positions that fit your expertise and interests. It also doesn't hurt to also attach a copy of your resume so they can pass it along to folks who may be interested in hiring you. Your network can be your most powerful ally in job searching before you leave your current job.

Tip 46: Get an Executive Coach

A coach is a good listener, asks powerful questions, and helps you learn how to find your own solutions. The good thing is that coaches are not just for executives. They can also help you move up to the next level by helping you identify habits and fears that may be holding you back. Why would you want to work with an executive coach?

Because you:

Want to grow as a person

Personal growth is an important part of moving forward in your career and enjoying your life. A coach can help you identify blind spots that may be limiting your success and happiness.

Are ready to move to the next level in your career

A coach can help you plan your next steps and identify how you create your own roadblocks to success. A coach can also help you role play interviews and help you identify which sort of organizations you want to work in next.

Want to increase your emotional intelligence

Self-awareness is one of the toughest skills to develop. They are very few people that are confident enough to tell you how others really view you. A coach helps you identify your blind spots when it comes to your self-perception and will help you develop strategies for your perception to match your reality.

You can find a coach through referrals from friends that have coaches and websites for accredited coaches. You may also want to contact coaching training programs. They often have students that are training to be professional coaches and will provided coaching services to you at a discounted rate. Coaches can be expensive, from $50-$500 an hour depending on their experience level. You may be able to make the case that coaching should be a part of your professional development budget. You can also make the case that coaching will prepare you for the next level of responsibility. You may already be connected to a coach through any fellowship or leadership development programs you are a part of.

If you are unable to find finding for a coach through work or through a fellowship, you might want to consider paying for it yourself. If your coach can help you move to the next level of responsibility faster or do a better job now, it is probably worth every penny of the fee that you will pay.

Ask a coach

Judy Ford is the founder of Sunrise Consulting, a firm that is focused on coaching social sector leaders. She was also Trista's executive coach when she first started her executive director position. Judy answers some of the common questions that you may have about working with an executive coach.

What will I do with my coach?

Think of coaching as a partnership, where the client and coach serve in different yet mutually important and critical roles in order for the partnership to succeed. The purpose of the partnership is to help clients: 1) achieve deeper learning about themselves; 2) identify their motivations as well as the things that serve as barriers or limitations for them; 3) identify their values and how those values operate for them in their lives; and 4) to use this and other information to help move the client toward action on issues and/or goals they determine will bring them greater fulfillment, better balance and a more effective process in their work and life in order to achieve the kind of success that holds deep meaning and value for the client.

The client's role is to be open and present for each coaching session and, in between coaching sessions, to actively put into practice in their lives and work the lessons learned during coaching. The clients also set the agenda for coaching — determine what they want to work on and the goals they want to achieve. Coaching is not a place where clients come simply to listen and be told what to do. Coaching is a process in which clients are guided into identifying and tapping into their own capacity for change and for accessing the answers to their own questions that they already possess. The coach's role is to serve as a patient listener, ask powerful questions and provide calm, reflective guidance that honors and supports the clients in accessing the revelations, answers and creative power for change they naturally embody.

Is this like therapy?

Coaching is not therapy. The therapist's role is that of 'expert,' with the responsibility for both diagnosing the client's 'problem' and prescribing treatment. In coaching, unlike therapy, it is the client, not the coach, who is the expert on the client's life. In coaching, it is the client who identifies the issue to work on during coaching and sets the agenda for the coaching process, and ultimately it is the client who comes up with the answers to the questions they have and the plan of action to achieve the goals they have set.

How often do we talk?

The process for coaching varies with coaches and clients, based on the client's needs and the coach's methodology. Some clients speak with their coach once per week. Others speak with their coach twice per month or only once per month. It all depends on the client's needs and what they work out in coordination with their coach. During the term of the coaching relationship, the number of times a client speaks with their coach can change — you can start off talking with your coach every week or twice per month and then move to speaking with your coach once per month, again based on your needs and how they might change over time.

Do we have to meet in person?

Some coaching practices only provide in-person coaching. Other coaching practices only conduct coaching by phone. Many coaching practices do some combination of the two. With today's technology, there are no "have-to's" in coaching where this is concerned. Coaching by phone is no more or less effective than coaching in-person and vice versa. It all depends on what the client's needs are and what they find most comfortable and conducive to their own learning and action.

Most of the coaching my company provides is done by telephone, which is both very effective and allows me to coach wonderful clients from all over the country. In addition, my very first executive coaching experience was conducted by phone once per month for an entire year while I was based in Maryland ... and my coach was based in Cape Town, South Africa! It was the most amazing and transformative experience, one that, in fact, led me to becoming a certified coach.

What sort of work should I do in between sessions?

The following is often heard throughout the coaching field: 'Coaching is what happens in between sessions.' This simply means that what is accomplished within the coaching session is setting the stage for what the client is responsible for applying to/enacting in their life in between the sessions. In my practice, homework for a client could be anything from recommended reading; an activity, class, workshop or seminar; a written exercise; a survey or interview; journaling; visioning; a meditation; an affirmation; or anything else that comes up during the session that the client feels will support their movement and action toward achieving their goals.

What sort of issues do coaches help with?

Coaches work with their clients on a wide variety of issues. There are coaches who specialize in any number of areas including: leadership development, organizational systems, relationships, education, health care, social action, adolescents/youth, spirituality, women/women as leaders, creativity/arts/culture, and, of course, the social benefit sector. Within these specialty areas, coaches can work with clients on any of the full breadth of issues that can potentially come up related to self-improvement, work/life balance, goal-setting, life/work changes, and overall desires for more fulfillment, achievement, and success. In my practice, I provide life coaching for individual clients and holistic, executive coaching and leadership development for leaders in the social benefit sector. In working with my clients, the issues we often work on include: values clarification; goal-setting; identifying and breaking through roadblocks; self-assessment/self-awareness skill building; situational analysis; visioning and reflection; relationship evaluation; work/life balance; voice-work/effective communication; restorative problem solving; life purpose; and mission identification.

How long will I need coaching?

Generally, for individual clients who voluntarily seek out coaching on their own, the coaching term is determined by the client, in consultation with their coach. Coaching is typically concluded based on either reaching the time allotted for coaching or when the client has determined that they have achieved through coaching what they came to coaching for. Should new needs or goals be determined during the initial coaching term, clients can always request additional coaching time or an extension of the coaching term. It is important to keep in mind that many coaches have minimum requirements for a coaching term based on the minimum timeframe necessary for reasonable results to be achieved by the client (generally, no less than three months).

Tip 47: Know When to Take the Leap

When it comes to taking the leap from one job to the next, some people need to pulled out of their current position with a crowbar and other people have a stack of resumes ready to go in their desk drawer. There are positive reasons to leave a job, such as if you have grown so much that you are ready to move on to the next level. There are also not-so-positive reasons to leave a job, like if you don't leave your job you'll suffocate from the boredom of it all. Here are some questions you should ask yourself before you take the leap:

Do you have 80% proficiency?

If you wait until you know how to do 100% of the things in your job perfectly, you will never actually leave. If you leave when you hardly know how to do your job, you probably haven't yet gotten enough out of the position. Shoot for 80% before you move on to the next job.

Is there room to grow in your organization?

Sometimes you don't have to move far to get additional responsibility. Look around your organization and see if your dream job is actually just down the hall. If you think that there is potential to move up talk to your supervisor or the organization's executive director and let them know that you are looking for a promotion.

Is there something you're running from?

Sometimes a challenge in your current position sends you running for the help wanted ads. Look closely at the situation to determine if you would gain more from dealing with the situation head on, rather than running away to another organization. Sometimes those problems have a way of following you from organization to organization if you don't see your part in creating the problem.

Do you dread going to work?

If you wake up every morning with a feeling of dread in the pit of your stomach, you are not doing yourself or your organization any favors by sticking around. Figure out what is causing your dread and when you take a new position make sure that you are not stepping into that same minefield.

It's important to be thoughtful about career changes, but sometimes you just have to take a leap of faith.

Don't get stuck in the admin pigeonhole

Especially for recent graduates moving into the nonprofit sector, it's important not to get stuck in the administrative track, if that's not where you want to be permanently. For many potential employers, if your background is purely administrative, they may have a hard time seeing how you would fit into other positions. Make sure that you vary your experiences with stretch assignments either in your current job or in your volunteer work.

Nonprofit Rockstar: Maria Cote

Maria Cote is someone who has figured out how to not get stuck in the administrative pigeonhole. After she graduated from college with a degree in Cultural Studies and Comparative Literature, she quickly discovered that her work experience, more than her education, would most strongly impact her job search. Her first position was serving as an office manager at Minnesota Housing Partnership (MHP), an intermediary nonprofit organization providing grants and loans for statewide affordable housing projects. She was responsible for information technology, website administration, human resources, and board support, among other administrative tasks.

When a position opened up for a communications and operations coordinator position at then four-year-old Admission Possible in St. Paul, Maria was able to apply the skills she'd learned in her two years at MHP to bring crucial expertise to this young nonprofit organization. As the fifth full-time staff member, she was able to lead a variety of strategic communications, fundraising, and operations initiatives to move Admission Possible from start-up phase into a more mature organization. As the organization continued to grow, Maria's original position split into several, allowing her to continually be promoted and become more specialized. Six years later, Maria is the senior development officer for institutional giving and development operations, and helping to lay the ground work for Admission Possible's efforts to help low-income students nationwide earn admission and graduate from college.

Tip 48: Resign Gracefully

Sometimes, you start a great nonprofit job, and it's just not what you expected. Maybe you really love the cause, but it's the organization itself that's driving you crazy. You enjoy working with the kids or doing outreach for the homeless, but you don't think you can go one more day working for your jerk of a boss. They don't pay you enough to deal with such dysfunction. Also, your friends are tired of your complaining. It may be time to quit, but we want to make sure you leave on good terms. Even if it *was* the nonprofit job from hell.

Write a formal resignation letter

Keep it short and to the point. Leave emotions out of it. Make sure you give the effective date of your resignation. As much as you may want to vent and rant about all the injustices done to you, this is just not the venue for that. Avoid putting in details of why you're leaving in the formal letter. Though it's supposed to be confidential, the reality is that anything you put in writing can be shared with anyone who happens upon your employee file later. If you really do have a grievance to pursue, use the appropriate channels outlined in the employee handbook.

Deliver the news in person

Request a meeting with your boss to "discuss your future with the organization." Nothing more needs to be said here. They will have an idea of what you want to meet about. Again, keep this meeting short and to the point — 30 minutes max. Begin by telling them how much you've appreciated the opportunity to serve the organization, but it's time for you to move on. You can insert whatever explanation you want here — you're leaving to pursue advancement opportunities elsewhere, going back to school, expand your experience with other nonprofits, etc. Whatever you do, don't say, "I'm leaving because you are certifiably insane and if I work here one more day I will jump out of a window." At the end of the meeting, give your boss the resignation letter that you've already prepared ahead of time.

Give at least two weeks' notice

If it's hard to get out of bed in the morning for a job you have grown to despise, this piece of advice can be a challenge. Especially when all you want to do is scream, "You can't fire me — I quit!" at the top of your lungs. But you must do this. It is a generally accepted professional courtesy to give your employer at least two weeks to find your replacement. This will also give you time to wrap up any projects to hand off to the next employee or delegate to one of your colleagues.

Write a positive farewell email to your stakeholders and colleagues

During your last days of work, be sure to inform those you've been working with for the last months or years. It's a courtesy to your colleagues to let them know that you're leaving the organization and where they can contact you in the future. Say something like, "I've learned a lot during my time at Toys for Toddlers, but I'm moving on to a new stage in my career. I appreciate having the opportunity to work with all of you, and I hope we can stay in touch ..."

Again, even if you're quitting on bad terms, just try to be as cordial and professional as possible. It's a small nonprofit world. If you leave any organization in a huff, people will be talking about you, and not in a good way.

Tip 49: Be a Good Manager

So you've built your skills, worked your network, knocked the interview out of the park, and ta-da, you are now a manager. Now what? You don't want to be the living example of the Peter Principle, which is described as "being promoted to your level of incompetence." So you better do a good job. Management guru Scott Berkun points out:

"On the day your job title includes 'manager' others depend on you. They will look to you for leadership, guidance, or advice. They may rely on you for career direction and job security. You have more influence on their happiness, and success than most people in their lives. The psychology and responsibility of managing others is complex and should be taken seriously."

Here are some steps to increase your success as a manager:

Get started on the right foot

We highly recommend the book *The First 90 Days* by Michael Watkins. The author gives great advice for laying a framework for success in your position.

Get to know what your staff really does

Although you don't need to master every task your staff handles, you need to understand their workload and responsibilities. You build the respect of your team if you understand their pressures and limitations.

Be a coach

The coach doesn't grab the ball during the game and take a shot. Your job is to help staff do their best and get out of the way so that they can perform. If you did that same position before you were promoted, you must be extra vigilant so that you don't start trying to do *their* job, instead of your own.

Help them move up

Too many managers are worried that if their staff members are too successful, they'll start trying to get the manager's job. Good. You want a staff that is so talented that any of them would be capable of running your department or your organization. Help your staff members develop their professional skills and ask them what they want to do next. You'll have a more dedicated staff and a stronger team.

Know your weaknesses as a manager

You can either fix those weaknesses or hire someone smarter than you to fill those gaps. Both strategies work, but ignoring your weaknesses is not an option. An executive coach or a trusted mentor can help you identify your weaknesses.

Give feedback early and often

Be sure your staff knows what they are doing well and what needs improvement. You should do this in both casual conversations and formal performance reviews. If someone isn't meeting your expectations, make sure that they know what your expectations are. Sometimes the issue is that you are not being direct and clear when giving assignments.

Let your employees make critical decisions

Give your staff permission to make decisions and don't second-guess them. If you train your employees well, you should believe that they will make good decisions in the best interest of your organization. Even if they make a different decision than you would have, you still need to have their back; otherwise all decisions will start to go through you and you become an organizational bottleneck.

Find your management mentors

Keep a confidential file (at home) with notes about strong managers you have worked with and bad managers you worked with. What were the specific things that you loved or drove you crazy? This helps you to not repeat those same mistakes. Even fictional characters can be management mentors or cautionary tales. Michael Scott from the television show "The Office" is a constant reminder of what *not* to do.

The bottom line is, you can't succeed as a manager if your team isn't successful. CompassPoint Nonprofit Services has made this definition clear. They say that the ultimate responsibility of their supervisors is to "guide, support, and manage the relationship between the staff and the organization, so that each is successful." Give yourself the skills you need to be this bridge between the people and the organization.

Respecting your elders and conducting their performance reviews

During Trista's first attempt at managing an older worker, she was rebuffed shortly after the interview. The interviewee called her back and said that she would have to remove herself from consideration from the position because she couldn't see herself being supervised by someone Trista's age (Trista was 25 at the time). Trista recalls:

"Despite the fact that she wasn't my top candidate (and was only a few years older than me), my confidence was still shaken. Would I ever be taken seriously or would everyone see me as a fresh-out-of-grad-school rookie, even though I had more than 10 years of nonprofit employment experience at that point? I gave myself a little pep talk and offered the position to my first choice, who was older than me and more experienced in development, but was looking for a flexible position where she could use her fantastic grantwriting skills and not work 60 hours a week as a director of development. Once I fully understood that I had the skills needed to manage the department and could build on the expertise of my new hire to build our internal capability, I was able to be less self-conscious about the age thing."

Here are some tips if you are managing someone older than you:

Don't broadcast your age

Be proud of what you have accomplished in a short period of time but there is no need to rub your age in people's faces or say things like, "Wow, you're two years older than my mom." It lowers team morale and doesn't make you look like an emerging leader — it makes you look like a snotty kid.

Be willing to listen to the ideas of your older staff

Instead of thinking of people as "stuck in their ways," give them the benefit of the doubt and be willing to try things their way.

Find a mentor who has supervised older staff

Learn from their successes and mistakes so your staff members don't have to be your guinea pigs. Developing good management skills in general will help you better manage staff across multiple generations.

Tip 50: Run with the Big Dogs

Trista often shares the following story:

"In high school I considered myself quite a track runner. Unfortunately that self-perception didn't match up to reality. I would always win my heat in sprints but I always ran in the slow heat because my coach thought I was lazy and not fast enough to run in the faster heats. I would think I did a great job in the 200 yard dash, beating the competition by two or three strides, but when my time was compared to the faster heats I would never even place in the top six, reinforcing my coach's belief that I stunk. During the city finals, I was lining up with my (slow) heat when the fastest girl on my team started to chicken out about running in the fast heat. She was afraid that she would get beaten in front of everyone. I offered to give her my spot and she happily accepted. Before my coach had a chance to see, I took her spot and ran with the fastest girls in the city. I could hear my coach screaming at the top of his lungs as soon as I left the starting block, "What the hell are you doing in the fast heat?!" I saw how fast the girls were running and as they started pulling ahead of me I found strength from within and ran faster than I ever had before. I ended up placing second in the heat (I swear the first place winner had legs that can only come from steroid use)."

What does this have to do with your career? The two biggest challenges for you to move to the next level in your career is the ability to see yourself in that next role and for others to see you in that role. By running with the faster competition, Trista could see herself as a better runner and so could the spectators. It became a self-fulfilling prophesy. The same holds true for the company that you keep and the places you are seen in your career. Here's what Trista learned from that experience:

When an opportunity for you to reach beyond your comfort zone and ability level comes, take it.

Trista never would have done so well in the race if she had stayed where she was "supposed" to, and the same can be said about her career in philanthropy. Popular wisdom says that she "should" have waited another 10 years until she was "fully prepared" to begin looking for a job in philanthropy. But when a plum opportunity in the field presented itself, she decided to swallow her fear and go for it instead.

Run against the best

Running with the slow heats made Trista lazy and complacent because she knew she was faster than her immediate competition. She wasn't doing her best because she didn't have the best to compare herself to. Are you already the most successful person in your personal or professional network? Then you need to expand your network to include some of the best so that you rise to the challenge.

Ask for forgiveness, not permission

Sometimes, by doing something you could never get permission to do, you do better and your organization does better. Figure out what are the things that will get you fired and keep the rest open to possibility.

Second place is OK

A fairy tale ending would have been Trista winning the race and getting carried off by her teammates. In reality, she was eating the dust of the first-place winner and getting yelled at by her coach. Despite this, she was happy because she knew she'd done her best and was challenging herself to the limit. In the process, she also helped her team win some additional points. Moral of the story: You may not always win in the work you are trying to accomplish, but as long as you are doing what is truly your best, you can't go wrong!

Nonprofit Rockstar: Mary Galeti

Mary Galeti is someone who has mastered the art of running with the big dogs. As vice-chair of the Tecovas Foundation, 28-year-old Mary doesn't fit the serious, grey-haired profile of a "traditional" foundation trustee. She hasn't let that stop her from being active in local and national philanthropy circles.

Mary has been involved in her family's philanthropy for approximately 10 years, but has only been in leadership for four. Her grandmother, Carol Emeny, created the Tecovas Foundation in 1998 for the purpose of building the Amarillo Globe News Center for the Performing Arts. The plan was to have some money remaining to teach grandkids about the power of organized philanthropy to accomplish big community goals.

Unfortunately, as often happens, the plan had to change. Within four years, Mary's grandmother, mother, and aunt all passed away, leaving just one member of the second generation and the majority of the board of directors of the foundation under 30. Also, because of the way the estates were planned, the foundation was no longer as meager as had been intended, and with the performing arts center completed, the Tecovas Foundation could go in any direction that it wanted. That meant that Mary and her cousins had to be ready to step up.

The challenge to stepping up is you have to believe not only that you can do it, but that you have earned the right to be wherever you end up. Being a trustee seemed easy enough. At the end of the day, she got to spend time with her family and do good work. The image of the elderly trustee didn't seem to make sense, since their whole board was so young. It was hard getting used to the strange way that nonprofits would treat her, once they found it she was a trustee.

"It seems like there is over-eagerness, and a lack of sincerity, once someone from an organization finds out who you are," she notes.

As Mary got more involved in the family foundation, she became more interested in growing and learning in the field. She began attending seminars and reading blogs, all in an effort to be better at the work they were doing. Then she got invited to speak at a conference with her aunt to talk about generational transition in family foundations. Afterwards, she was invited to join the Council on Foundations Family Philanthropy Committee. It wasn't until that moment that she realized how rare her experience was.

Mary recalls the event: "I showed up to the first meeting in DC, and I didn't know anybody, really. I looked around the board table as everyone introduced themselves, many from foundations doing amazing and important work. I had no idea what I was doing in that room. No one really looked like me. I felt like I was the only one in the room who had come to the philanthropic community by way of family tragedy, and everyone would know that I didn't really belong. Luckily, I really like the sound of my own voice, so even though I was intimidated by the group, that didn't stop me from participating and sharing my thoughts."

That's when her biggest challenge became clear. No one else on the committee seemed to care that she was under 30 or how she got there. The only one who cared was Mary herself. Fundamentally, she had to be more comfortable with the fact that she was being invited to do participate in projects, committees and boards because she had something to offer — and it was more than just her demographic. Every now and again, she says she still needs the reminder.

Soon after, she served on the planning committee for the Family Philanthropy conference and co-chaired the same conference the following year. She became a Startingbloc fellow. She was invited to join boards and committees. She's had to learn how to decide how to spend her time and energy. She decided on three criteria: She has to like and want to learn from whom she would be working with; there has to be some aspect of the work that she's passionate about; and there has to be some aspect of the work that seems like it would push her boundaries, learning, and comfort zone.

"Making sure that whatever I'm involved in fits those criteria means that I'm being thoughtful about valuing my time," Mary says. "Being involved in the nonprofit world can mean an endless list of opportunities that have the potential to make you feel good and make change. I think it's important to make sure that the change you make doesn't just make the world better, it makes you better, too. Otherwise you end up burned out before you're 40."

Resources

Books You Should Totally Read

Here are some of our favorite books that expand on many of the concepts we've covered in *How to Become a Nonprofit Rockstar*.

Brand Yourself: How to Create an Identity for a Brilliant Career by David Andrusia and Rick Haskins

Made to Stick: Why Some Ideas Survive and Others Die by Chip Heath and Dan Heath

Me 2.0 by Dan Schawbel

Make a Name for Yourself: 8 Steps Every Woman Needs to Create a Personal Brand by Robin Fisher Roffer

The No Asshole Rule: Building a Civilized Workplace and Surviving One That Isn't by Robert I. Sutton

What Got You Here Won't Get You There: How Successful People Become Even More Successful by Marshall Goldsmith and Mark Reiter

Professional Associations Worth Joining

Nonprofit Professional Associations

Alliance for Nonprofit Management

The Alliance for Nonprofit Management is the professional association of individuals and organizations devoted to improving the management and governance capacity of nonprofits — to assist nonprofits in fulfilling their mission. http://www.allianceonline.org/

American Society for Public Administration (ASPA)

The American Society for Public Administration is the nation's most respected society representing all forums in the public service arena including the nonprofit sector. http://www.aspanet.org/scriptcontent/index.cfm

Association of Fundraising Professionals (AFP)

The Association of Fundraising Professionals (AFP) represents nearly 28,000 members in more than 190 chapters throughout the world, working to advance philanthropy through advocacy, research, education, and certification programs. http://www.afpnet.org/

Association for Research on Nonprofit Organizations and Voluntary Action (ARNOVA)

ARNOVA is an international membership organization dedicated to fostering through research an understanding of the nonprofit sector, philanthropy and volunteerism. http://www.arnova.org/

Grant Professionals Network (GPN)

The Grant Professionals Network provides a collegial forum to facilitate training, resource development, leadership, and networking opportunities for grant professionals. http://www.gpninc.org/

National Council of Nonprofit Associations

The National Council of Nonprofit Associations (NCNA) is the network of state and regional nonprofit associations serving over 20,000 members in 41 states and the District of Columbia. http://www.ncna.org/

Society for Nonprofit Organizations

With a 25-year history and over 6,000 members, the Society for Nonprofit Organizations is one of the oldest and largest nonprofit management support organizations in the country. http://www.snpo.org/

Young Nonprofit Professionals Network (YNPN)

The Young Nonprofit Professionals Network (YNPN) is a powerful, organic vehicle for retaining and strengthening the nonprofit sector's next generation of leaders — led by and directly responsive to the needs of early career nonprofit professionals. http://www.ynpn.org/

Philanthropic Professional Associations

Association of Black Foundation Executives

The Association of Black Foundation Executives (ABFE) was established in 1971 by forward-thinking, black foundation executives to promote effective and responsive philanthropy in black communities. http://www.abfe.org

Asian Americans/Pacific Islanders in Philanthropy

AAPIP is a national membership and philanthropic advocacy organization dedicated to advancing philanthropy and Asian American/Pacific Islander (AAPI) communities. Our members include foundations, staff and trustees of grantmaking institutions, and nonprofit organizations in regional chapters throughout the United States. http://www.aapip.org

Emerging Practitioners in Philanthropy

The mission of Emerging Practitioners in Philanthropy (EPIP) is to strengthen the next generation of grantmakers in order to advance effective social justice philanthropy. EPIP is a national funder network composed of grantmakers, trustees, staff at Regional Associations and Affinity Groups, and graduate students studying philanthropy. The network was organized to serve staff under the age of 40, those new to the grantmaking field, and/or those in junior positions. http://www.epip.org

Funders for Lesbian and Gay Issues

Funders for Lesbian and Gay Issues seeks equality and rights for lesbian, gay, bisexual, transgender, and queer individuals and communities by mobilizing philanthropic resources that advance racial, economic, and gender justice. http://www.lgbtfunders.org

Hispanics in Philanthropy

Hispanics in Philanthropy is committed to strengthening Latino communities by increasing resources for the Latino and Latin American civil sector and by increasing Latino participation and leadership throughout the field of philanthropy. http://www.hiponline.org

Jewish Funders Network

Jewish Funders Network is an organization of individual and institutional grantmakers committed to broadening the base and scope of Jewish philanthropy and advancing its effective practice. http://www.jfunders.org

Native Americans in Philanthropy

The mission of Native Americans in Philanthropy is to advance philanthropic practices grounded in native values and traditions. http://www.nativephilanthropy.org

Neighborhood Funders Group

The Neighborhood Funders Group is a membership association of grantmaking institutions. It's their mission to strengthen the capacity of organized philanthropy to understand and support community-based efforts to organize and improve the economic and social fabric of low-income urban neighborhoods and rural communities. http://www.nfg.org

Women's Funding Network

Women's Funding Network, a partnership of women's funds, donors, and allies around the world committed to social justice, works to ensure that women's funds are recognized as the "investment of choice" for people who value the full participation of women and girls as key to strong, equitable and sustainable communities and societies. http://www.wfnet.org

Foundation and Nonprofit Fellowships We Love

Foundation Fellowships

Association of Black Foundation Executives (ABFE)

Connecting Leaders Fellowship Program

The program is a yearlong experience designed to sharpen the skills and strengthen the leadership capacity of foundation staff, donors, and trustees who are committed to assisting black communities through philanthropy. Fellows will have the opportunity to learn from seasoned grantmakers on a regular basis, understand how to be more effective change agents within their institutions, and participate in a network that focuses on innovative solutions to community challenges. Each fellow will be assigned a leadership coach as part of the program. Fellows receive a stipend in support of their professional development.

http://www.abfe.org

Center on Philanthropy and Civil Society

Emerging Leaders International Fellows Program

The Center on Philanthropy and Civil Society's Emerging Leaders International Fellows Program provides leadership training through applied research and professional mentorships for young scholar-practitioners in the nonprofit sector. The program is open to scholars and practitioners interested in building Third-Sector capacity in the United States and overseas. Fellows are based at The Graduate Center of The City University of New York, where they design and pursue an individualized research project and participate in a seminar with Third-Sector leaders. Specific topical areas are chosen each year. Each fellowship covers the cost of tuition and includes a $1,300-per month stipend (less applicable taxes and fees) to cover living and research-related expenses. The Center will also provide single-room dormitory accommodations with shared facilities at

International House (adjacent to Columbia University), as well as economy round-trip air travel to and from New York City.

http://www.philanthropy.org/programs/intnl_fellows_program.html

Emerging Practitioners in Philanthropy

Professional Development Fund

Designed to increase access to professional development conferences and trainings for emerging philanthropic practitioners, with an emphasis on supporting the leadership and the retention of young people of color in the field, the PDF will provide partial funding for recipients to participate in one professional conference or training in the foundation field. Examples of appropriate conferences and trainings include, but are not limited to: Affinity Group or Regional Associations of Grantmakers conferences; Council on Foundations conferences (Annual, Family, or Community Foundations) or institutes (for New Grantmakers or Trustees); trainings by philanthropy advocacy groups (such as Alliance for Justice); and grantmaker education trainings (such as The Grantmaking School or GrantCraft). In addition to helping participants attend their conference of choice, EPIP will provide a gathering for all Fund recipients so that they meet one another and other peers, gain value from EPIP's internal professional development programs, and learn more about resources available across the field.

http://www.epip.org

Nonprofit Fellowships

Ashoka Fellows

International organization Ashoka offers up to 25 three-year fellowships for "social entrepreneurs" — individuals who wish to create or expand public-service projects — that include stipends based on financial need (up to $55,000 per year) and access to pro bono management and leadership assistance. Ashoka also facilitates international collaborations among its fellows.

http://www.ashoka.org/fellows

Coro Foundation

Coro Fellows Program in Public Affairs

Coro, with offices in Los Angeles, New York, Pittsburgh, San Francisco, and St. Louis, offers full-time, nine-month fellowships that include field assignments, individual and group projects, and a formal relationship with a mentor. Tuition is $3,500, though scholarships and living-expenses assistance are available on a case-by-case basis.

http://www.coro.org

Echoing Green

Echoing Green Fellowships

Each year, the Echoing Green Foundation, in New York, offers 20 "social entrepreneurs" stipends of up to $90,000 over two years, health benefits, and management support to complete or expand public service projects.

http://www.echoinggreen.org

Indiana University

The Fund Raising School

Reach new levels of fundraising success. The School teaches the historical and philanthropic context, the current issues, and the art and science of fundraising and philanthropy. You gain the knowledge needed to build your organization's resources with confidence and success in an ever-changing society. Available courses include Basic Elements of Fundraising, Planned Giving, Managing a Capital Campaign, and Board Development. Partial scholarships are available.

http://www.philanthropy.iupui.edu

The New World Foundation

The Alston/Bannerman Fellowship Program

A $15,000 grant provides funding for a three-month (or longer) sabbatical for activists of color. Open to people of color, living in the United States, with a minimum of 10 years experience, who have been committed to social change.

http://www.alstonbannerman.org/

The Draper Richards Foundation

Social Entrepreneur Fellowship

This provides selected social entrepreneurs with funding of $100,000 annually for three years. The funds are specifically and solely for entrepreneurs starting new nonprofit organizations. The Draper Richards Fellowships are highly selective, with only six fellows selected each year.

http://www.draperrichards.org

Rockefeller Foundation

Bellagio Public Affairs Residencies

Residencies are for policy makers, non-governmental organization practitioners, social entrepreneurs, activists, individuals from the corporate sector engaged in social investment projects, and journalists. They provide time for critical thinking, disciplined work, individual reflection, and collegial engagement, uninterrupted by the usual professional and personal demands. The Foundation also encourages demonstrated leaders to use time at Bellagio for reflection and repositioning of their organizations in a rapidly changing world. The Center typically offers two- to four-week residencies for up to three public affairs professionals at a time. The professional work of an applicant must align with the Foundation's mission to expand opportunities for poor or vulnerable people and to help ensure that globalization's benefits are shared more widely. The fellowship covers room and board at the Bellagio study and conference center in Italy.

http://www.rockfound.org/bellagio/bellagio.shtml

Bring the Nonprofit Rockstar Tour
to Your Town

Rosetta Thurman and Trista Harris are available to come to your city for book signings and events. Rosetta and Trista are both skilled at providing unique, inspiring and effective keynotes and presentations for audiences of all sizes. Want to book the authors for an event, conference, workshop or book signing? Email Rosetta at rosetta@rosettathurman.com or Trista at speaking@tristaharris.com with your request.

The authors are available for the following opportunities:

- **Speaking:** The authors frequently speak to audiences of all sizes about the themes highlighted in the book. Rosetta and Trista can tailor their presentation to your specific audience and the desired outcomes of the event.

- **Workshops:** The authors are known for delivering fun, highly interactive sessions for groups of all sizes.

- **Customized Training Sessions:** The authors can also deliver 1/2 day or full-day sessions tailored to your particular event or audience that will help them apply the 50 tips to their careers, with ample time for one-on-one discussion and facilitated peer learning.

Made in the USA
Lexington, KY
14 November 2012